LIFE IN THE SLOW LANE

J. P. HART

This is a work of fiction. Names, characters, places and incidents either are a product of the author's imagination or used factiously and any resemblance to actual persons living or dead, businesses establishments, events or locales is entirely coincidental.

PROLOGUE

He liked to preach; at least that is what he told himself. He thought you could save a soul by preaching at it more than praying for it.

He thought being a priest would be the way to go. After all he had all the indoctrination, Catholic grammar school, high school, altar boy, mass on Sundays, daily mass, holy days, fasting, abstaining, penance, retreats, novenas, patron saints, praying for the living, the sick, the dying, the dead, sacrificing, praying the rosary, the litanies, the relics, the nine First Fridays, the five First Saturdays, praying for vocations, for the conversion of Russia, the Ten Commandments, the Eight Beatitudes, the Seven Deadly Sins, the Seven Sacraments, The six Precepts of the Church, the Four Cardinal virtues, Original Sin, Mortal Sin, Venial Sin, the near occasion of sin, Heaven, Hell, Purgatory, Limbo, the Spiritual works of Mercy, the Corporal Works of Mercy, the Seven Gifts of the Holy Ghost, nine ways to be an accessory to another person's sins, the brochures and the everlasting guilt, Amen

In the seminary he was not the best student as he had a short attention span and it was a struggle to get thru many of the classes. Actually he was last in his class though it was only a class of four, as very few were becoming priests, it was still last. He figured someone had to be last and it might as well be him, he didn't care. He wasn't in it to become Pope.

When he was ordained his parents were quite proud and when he gave his first sermon he rambled but it didn't matter to him, he was doing what he always dreamed of doing.

Then the tedium set in and eventually he was on the outside looking in.

ONE

Muldoon was sitting at his desk daydreaming when he heard what sounded like whimpering coming from Roundtree's cubicle.

Muldoon got up and looked over the cubicle wall that separated their workspaces and saw Roundtree hunched over his desk.

Roundtree had just hung up his phone. He looked up and saw Muldoon. "That was Annie", he said, "Our son has been accepted into law school."

"That is depressing." Muldoon said.

"It means we have failed as parents."

Muldoon had nothing to say. He looked at Roundtree who appeared to be overcome with grief, "maybe he won't pass the bar," Muldoon said hoping to pick up Roundtree's spirits.

"Why would he want to go through life a lawyer? Why would anyone want to see guilty people go free just to make a few bucks and sue for no valid reasons?" He looked at Muldoon with the saddest eyes Muldoon had ever seen.

"Well, I'm not paying for it." Roundtree said He liked to preach; at least that is what he told himself. He thought you could save a soul by preaching at it more than praying for it.

"That's the spirit." Muldoon said.

"I could just kill him and so could Annie."

"I wouldn't think you'd have to go that far. It's not like he is becoming a TV Weatherman."

"Well they're useless as well." Roundtree looked around. "I'm taking the rest of the day off." He got up and grabbed his sports coat that was hanging over a chair and walked out of the office.

Muldoon watched him leave then went back to daydreaming. He had a pile of files on his desk that he was supposed to be reviewing. They were to his right. There was a PC in front of him. To his left was a work area and then the opening to his cubicle. Muldoon looked through the opening and saw nothing but a dull, gray fall day. He was told he was lucky; he had a cubicle that was next to the windows. If he got up and walked over to the windows he could look down on a parking lot and to the gridlock of downtown Chicago.

He wasn't actually daydreaming, as his mind was actually blank, just how he liked it. It was Monday, the Bears had lost yesterday, so there would be a lot of whining. Muldoon didn't care to listen to it, which was why he was in his cubicle instead of wandering aimlessly about the office wondering if there would ever be a day that the Bears would have a quarterback. He knew there wouldn't and he knew he should try to get some work done, at least shuffle some papers, but he wasn't even up to that.

The World Series was also going on, but last night's game was an extra inning affair that went on forever. Muldoon had made it to the eleventh inning then packed it in.

Muldoon worked for Consolidated Metropolitan Insurance, known as CMI. Muldoon was Casualty Underwriting Supervisor. Not even Muldoon knew what that meant, as he didn't really know whom or what he was supposed to be supervising, perhaps Roundtree, but Roundtree had left the building. But the title looked and sounded impressive, which in insurance is pretty much the name of the game.

"You see the Jensen file?"

Muldoon looked up and saw Joe Tucker, the semi illiterate Branch Manager standing at his cubicle. "I gave it to you Friday."

"When?'

"Friday. You were on the phone when I dropped it off on your desk."

Tucker looked at the ceiling as if in deep thought, "I was on the phone all day Friday."

"Well, that's when I gave it to you."

"Morning or afternoon?"

"Afternoon."

Tucker was perplexed. There were many days he would be on the phone the entire day, but not talking to anyone. He would take the phone off the hook and hold it to his ear as if he was having some high level conversation when in truth he was trying to decide if he should have an ear pierced. CMI had just named a new president, J. Allen Ritchie, and it was reported he was gay. Tucker figured a good ear piercing might send him zooming up the corporate ladder.

The only problem, he wasn't sure what ear he should have pierced. Tucker was not good at making decisions. He didn't want to pierce a body part and then find out it wasn't necessary.

"When I was on the phone was I talking to any one?" Tucker asked.

"I assume that is what one does on the phone."

"You should know by now Larry that you should never assume anything in this business." He turned and slowly walked away while rubbing his left ear lobe.

Muldoon watched him go. Muldoon remembered the time he enjoyed working for Joe Tucker. That was back when Muldoon was a good company man. Back when he would come in early and stay late and even work an occasional Saturday morning. He did this all for the honor and glory of CMI as he never received any extra pay for this extra time. Then CMI had what they called a bad year, only made 200 million. So they froze everyone's salary and cut 15% of the work force. It was then that Muldoon figured that if a multi-billion-dollar corporation couldn't give raises it didn't deserve

9

anything from him. So he stopped coming in early and staying late and never worked another Saturday morning.

One day Tucker called Muldoon into his office, "can't give you a Christmas bonus this year Larry."

"Why not?"

"Because you don't come in early or stay late."

"I don't get paid to come in early or stay late."

"But the work has to get done."

"Bit it does get done."

"But it doesn't get done early or late. It gets done during normal business hours."

"And what's wrong with that?"

"Everything. We have people putting in 45-60 hours a week and they get no more done than you do. How do you think that looks to the people in the Home Office?"

"Good?" Muldoon said.

"Terrible," Tucker said. "In order to have a successful company everyone must either be efficient or inefficient. Seeing that the majority are inefficient you should comply with the norm. You're making a lot of people nervous by being efficient."

"What can I do to help?" Muldoon wondered.

"Screw up. Don't do your job in 40 hours. On occasion take 60. Take work home with you on weekends and bring it back undone. Appearances Larry are important. Take my advice and start screwing up and you can rise right to the top. It's not what you do that is important it is what people think you are doing that is important."

Muldoon said, "I thought the cubicles were installed to make us more efficient so we could do more."

"They were?" Tucker was alarmed by this piece of news.

"I thought so."

"Where did you hear that rumor?"

"It was in a memo."

Now Tucker was concerned, "no one reads those damn things. For god's sake Larry don't tell me you read those damn things. It's bad enough you get your work done in 40 hours, you don't read those goddam memos too."

"On occasion," Muldoon said trying to make it sound as if he only read them when there was absolutely nothing else to do, which was indeed when he read them.

"Well cease and desist or I won't be able to get you a raise this year."

"But you are not getting me a raise this year."

"And don't you forget it."

Then last Thursday Tucker called Muldoon into his office. Tucker was quite friendly, was wearing his power blue business suit, had a big toothy grin, offered Muldoon a chair and asked, "How would you like to be the Underwriting Manager of our Omaha Office. You know they are supposed to have a nice zoo there."

"In our office?"

"No, in Omaha."

"They do?"

"That is what I am told, has animals and everything."

"You sure?"

"Not really, but every city has a zoo. It's a rule of some kind."

"Really?"

"I'm told it is."

"Why me?"

"Why you what?"

"Why am I being offered the job?"

Tucker looked across his desk at Muldoon. He wanted Muldoon to take the job. Omaha was only about 500 miles from Chicago but that would be far enough. He wanted Muldoon out of his hair. His efficiency was getting to Tucker. Muldoon was getting more done in 3 hours than most were getting done in 12. People were starting to notice. People above Tucker. CMI had a new corporate strategy, it was called *Corporate Efficiency.* Something a suit with too much time on his hands thought up. It was a concept Tucker found appalling.

By promoting him Tucker could have Muldoon out of his hair and Tucker could go back to having a nice lackadaisical office that made a few bucks for the company, and he wouldn't have to worry about anyone being efficient. Tucker firmly believed that efficiency could very well be the root of all evil.

By having Muldoon promoted he could also take credit for it by letting the word out that due to the excellent supervision and training Muldoon had received while in the Chicago Muldoon was the perfect choice. Then when Muldoon did a good job, which he no doubt would, some of the credit would rub off on Tucker. Tucker rubbed his right ear lobe, "you're being offered this Larry as you are a good man and CMI likes good men and good men are hard to find, but lo and behold we have one in you."

"I thought I was too efficient to get ahead."

"Whoever said that?"

"You did."

"Larry you should never listen to anything I say. I know I don't."

"Then how do you know what you say?"

"About what?"

"About anything."

"I don't. Where were we?"

"Omaha."

"Oh yeah, the town with the zoo. This would be a great opportunity Larry." Tucker got up from behind his desk and walked over to the window. Tucker knew CMI was looking for a new Underwriting Manager for Omaha, and any promotion would have to come out of the Home Office but Tucker knew that Muldoon was well regarded by them. Tucker might be getting ahead of himself but he felt sure that if he recommended Muldoon for the job the chances would be pretty good it would be accepted. "You get a chance to move up the old corporate ladder, make a few bucks and get away from the all the damn taxes we have here." Tucker said.

Muldoon was hearing but not listening, or perhaps it was the other way around. Joe Tucker was the man who proved the validity of The Peter Principle that everyone rises to his or her level of incompetence. Tucker had not only reached his level, but left it in the dust.

Muldoon wasn't sure if he knew where Omaha was. He knew it was in Nebraska, but that was about it. And talking with Tucker could be trying as Tucker had the attention span of a gnat and rarely made sense, but Muldoon forged ahead. "Don't they have taxes in Omaha?"

"I'm sure they do."

"So what would be the advantage?"

Tucker thought for a minute then answered, "The zoo." Tucker believed this was an excellent answer, and then added, "That guy Marlin Perkins who use to be on TV for that insurance company discovered it."

Muldoon didn't say anything at first, as he didn't know Marlin Perkins, "He discovered Omaha?"

"No the damn zoo. Marlin was like the Crocodile Hunter of his day but better than that guy. Marlin Perkins would run rings around the Crocodile Hunter. Unfortunately they are both dead. "Why I once saw him wrestle an anaconda and hell he was about 80 years old. I yelled at the TV for the cameraman to drop the damn camera and save Marlin for I thought Marlin was going meet his maker right then and there. But old Marlin wrestled that damn snake down and then sold the country some health insurance."

"Sounds like quite the guy."

"An American original and he was happy in Omaha, just like you would be."

Muldoon looked at Tucker and could only wonder, wonder what the world was coming to. Tucker was an idiot. He was making the big bucks and the man was an idiot. Muldoon watched Tucker play with his ear and asked, "why not offer the job to Bernie?"

"Bernie who?"

"You know Bernie, *our* underwriting manager."

"Larry don't go stupid on me," Tucker was appalled by the suggestion. "Why would Bernie want to go to Omaha? Hell, Bernie likes the big city. He even goes to the theater. Can you believe that, the fucking theater? You know all these people who say they love living in Chicago? They always say one of the reasons is they love the theater, yet they never go. But Bernie goes. If we sent Bernie to Omaha he would think that it was too small. Plus Bernie is," Tucker looked around the office as if someone might overhear what he had to say, "stupid."

"Yeah. But Bernie deserves a step down simply because he is stupid."

Tucker returned from the window after staring at something down below and started to rub his left lobe. "Larry when are you going to understand the corporate structure. The higher you go and the more inefficient you are the larger the office you have. You see Larry, large offices run by themselves, but small offices need people. People who are smart. People like you. Now if you were to go to Omaha and fuck up, you'd be back here before you could say

18

Jack Robinson, but if you go to Omaha and do a good job, you can die there." Tucker smiled.

"What is in it for me?"

Tucker hadn't thought this far ahead but answered anyway, "If you accept the promotion you get a raise, I'd say in the neighborhood of twenty percent. All your moving expenses would be paid. If you buy a house in Omaha the company will pay the closing costs. We'll pay for any living expense you may have while you're in Omaha and the rest of the family is here. This is a real opportunity for you Larry." Tucker didn't know if any of this was true but it sounded good. And in insurance sounding good was half the battle.

Muldoon sat silent for a few moments. He would like to be an Underwriting Manager, but he didn't know if he wanted to be one in Omaha. He didn't know a thing about Omaha, other than it was in Nebraska. He thought of his wife, Sarah, and the kids. What would they think? Would they want to go? What about his house here? Could he sell it? Would he be able to buy another one? Would he be able to afford one?

Suddenly things seemed to be moving too fast for Muldoon. He wanted to get ahead, but did he want to move? And there were other people who were in a better position to move who were just as qualified as Muldoon. Money was important to Muldoon but it wasn't *that* important. He wanted a raise but he didn't know if he wanted to disrupt his family life for more money. He thought of Doris Simpson, CMI's Property Manager. She was qualified, in her mid-30's, single, smart, articulate and had the experience. Why hadn't Tucker offered it to her?

"What about Doris?" Muldoon said.

"What about her?"

"Why is she being passed over? Not that I'm trying to talk myself out of the job," Muldoon hedged, "but to me it would make more sense to send her to Omaha."

"Yeah, but she is a woman."

"What does that have to do with anything nowadays?"

"Nothing wrong with being a woman, but she is the wrong kind."

"She is? How many kinds are there?" Muldoon found that any conversation with Tucker could lead anywhere and take various unknown routes to get there.

"She's white and she's normal, doesn't have a prayer. If she was a black, pregnant foreign born who couldn't speak English and had 4-5 kids before the age of 12 by 4 different guys and no more than a fifth grade education she could rise right to the top. You know affirmative action and all that shit. I'll tell you something Larry," Tucker said as if letting Muldoon in on a big secret, "it doesn't pay to be white and normal. Hell it doesn't even pay to be black and normal anymore. If you want to get ahead you should be anything but white and anything but normal."

"I'm white and I consider myself normal." Muldoon said.

"Yeah, but you're efficient which is abnormal and a plus." Tucker pointed out to the office. "How many efficient people to you see out there? I'll tell you how many, none. Take Phillips, he sleeps."

Phillips was an underwriter who thought the main purpose of the cubicle, or workstations as those who like to think corporate call them, were made for naps.

"You know that?" Muldoon was somewhat surprised that Tucker actually knew something that went on in the office.

"The snoring alone gives it away, but he comes in on Saturdays. And you take Wanda the dip in charge of the clerical. She has been pregnant twice in the past two years, by two different men and neither one of them her husband. Her home life is so fucked up she could be executive material. Then there is Jasper one of our illustrious claims adjusters. Hasn't worked past 11:30 in six years. Spends his afternoons at that strip joint on Mannheim getting loaded."

"Then why are they still around?"

"Because it is damn near impossible to fire anyone who is a fuck up. If we got rid of Phillips the guy would go to the Labor

Relations Board and file an unfair labor grievance against us. If we try to dump Wanda she'd go on welfare, and then we'd have the local welfare agency looking at us, and if we fire Jasper for being a drunk we would be in trouble with the Americans With Disabilities Act. Anyway we'd be sued and we'd lose. So you see Larry what it all comes down to is you are vulnerable. You're normal."

"But you just said it doesn't pay to be normal."

"I did? I'm sorry I wasn't listening again. What it all boils down to Larry is if you go to Omaha and do a nice dependable job, you'll make a few extra bucks and you will be able to stay there for life," again Tucker smiled. "But if you ever screw up, or develop some real strange habits, or came up with a fucked up family life you'd be back here sooner than you think. And if you were to really go goofy you could go to the Home Office where there is nothing but abnormality."

"Is this a promotion?" Muldoon wondered.

"You're goddam right it is. You'll be in an office where you will be able to make the final decision. Sure, it is not the biggest of our offices, but all the same it is a nice office."

"What happens after Omaha?

"Beats me. If you like the city, do a good job you stay there. If you don't like it there simply fuck up and you can get to a larger office where your mistakes can be hidden."

Muldoon was numbed by what he was hearing. He felt that a promotion, or at least the offer of one, should make you feel good. But Muldoon didn't feel good. He only felt confused.

"Tell you what Larry," Tucker said, "think it over. I don't need an answer this minute Talk it over with the wife, your friends and remember one thing; *you have nothing to lose by going and nothing to gain by staying.* Take a ride over there and look at their zoo. It's supposed to be a nice zoo."

That was last week. Muldoon had talked about it with Sarah and asked the kids what they would think of moving to Omaha. They didn't care. Sarah was worried about what her parents would do but otherwise was willing. The kids, twin boys age 11 and a girl age 8 were really too young to worry about such things but did have the spirit of adventure in their bones.

Muldoon looked out from his cubicle and saw Fred Phillips walking by, "Say Fred, you got a minute?"

"Yeah," he yawned.

"You ever been to Omaha?"

"No, but I hear they have a nice zoo."

"Yeah, I've heard."

"Tucker offer you the job?"

"Yeah, how did you know?"

"There are no secrets here, you know that. Want a piece of advice Larry?"

"Sure."

"Take it."

"You think so?"

"Sure. Get out of this rat race. The damn congestion. Let me ask you, how long do you spend each day commuting?"

"A couple of hours or so."

"I bet in Omaha you could cut that in half or more without all the hassle or the expense. And another thing you probably wouldn't have to work on Saturdays."

"I don't now."

Phillips was surprised, "I didn't know that."

"Do you work on Saturdays?" Muldoon asked.

"No, but I come in."

"What for?"

"To read the paper and sleep which is probably why I never knew you weren't here."

"Can't you do that at home?"

"No. The kids drive me nuts and the wife always has some project she wants me to do. So I come in on Saturdays to get away from that shit."

"Thanks for the advice Fred."

"Sure, anytime."

Would be nice not to have to commute every day, but Muldoon didn't really mind the train ride though at times in the summer it became a drag. It did give him a chance to read the paper and if he couldn't read the paper on the train then he'd have to read it at home. So anytime saved by not commuting would be lost by having to read the paper at home.

Muldoon looked at the digital clock on his desk; it was time for his coffee break with the luscious Vicki Higgins in the claims department. Muldoon headed for the break room.

TWO

CMI offices occupied the fifth and sixth floor of a 24-story office building in the Loop. The break room was in a corner on the sixth floor with a view of the building across the street.

The break room looked like a kitchen. One wall had counter space with a sink built in and cabinets on either side of the sink. There was a microwave on the counter, which was mainly used for making popcorn and heating frozen lunches. Above this counter were more cabinets containing coffee cups, paper plates, napkins and other odds and ends that employees brought to work to share. At the end of the counter was a refrigerator. There were 7 round tables in the room with six chairs for each table. This was the main break room. There was a smaller one on the fifth floor.

There were not many people in the break room. About a year ago CMI instituted a policy of letting employees have coffee at their desks. For those who accepted this they would give up their morning and afternoon break. Many in the office went along with this with the exception of Phillips who needed his afternoon break to help him wake up. Vicki Higgins, who did both, had coffee at her desk and also took breaks. Muldoon always took breaks not only to see Vicki but if he drank coffee all day at his desk he'd spend the better part of the day in the men's room.

Muldoon entered the room hoping to come upon the luscious Vicki Higgins but instead found sitting in her usual spot Trevayne Robinson, CMI's original token black. Trevayne was hired in an affirmative action move as CMI thought this would be a good move, having a black on board. Though it took them almost 5 years to reach this decision it was considered a good corporate move. Now there were more blacks on board, as that train left the station quite awhile ago. He is now what CMI called a senior underwriter. No one really knew what that meant, least of all Trevayne Robinson.

Trevayne had opportunities to move up the corporate ladder with CMI but chose to stay where he was. He simply felt that additional responsibility and authority that a management position might offer simply wasn't worth it. There were some in the black community that thought Trevayne would make a good example of a successful black by simply moving up the corporate ladder. But these were your Jesse Jackson types that were always good at giving advice but poor at taking any and Trevayne was happy at where he was.

Plus, to get ahead you always had to kiss someone's ass, or put up with an ass. Life was simply too short for that type of bullshit. And now that Trevayne was closing in on retirement and simply didn't need the grief.

He and his wife lived in a bungalow on the south side of Chicago in a neighborhood known as Park Manor. They lived here for many years. Their kids were grown and gone and he and his wife now had a nice simple life. As long as Trevayne stayed black and dependable he could have a job for life.

"You be here looking for the luscious Vicki Higgins?" Trevayne asked in his jive jig talk he would use to make sure no one forgot he was black, as if that was possible. Vicki was always referred to as *the luscious Vicki Higgins* especially when she wasn't around. All the men thought she was luscious, Trevayne even remarked one day that she was the finest looking white woman he had ever seen "even better than Whitney Houston on a good day."

"Was hoping to find her, but as you can see my luck is not running too good." Muldoon said while walking over to the coffee pot

"Sorry to disappoint you." Trevayne was not only black, but also a big portly man with a beard he kept well-trimmed. He was over six feet tall and weighed in at 250 pounds. Not at all luscious looking unless you were a big portly black woman. "Going to Omaha, the most segregated city in America?"

"Where did you hear that?"

"Everyone knows it is."

"I mean about me being offered the job."

"Things get around."

Muldoon was standing at the coffeepot pouring a cup of black coffee. "What makes you think Omaha is more segregated than here?"

"It isn't. We just be saying that about every city that has itself a white Mayor, puts a lot of you people on a guilt trip."

"I don't feel guilty."

"Some day you will, after we repeat to you about a thousand times."

"I thought you already had," Muldoon sat across from Trevayne, "Seriously would you go?"

"They're supposed to have a nice zoo."

Muldoon let out a sigh, "anything else?"

"Not that I'm aware of."

The luscious Vicki Higgins then entered the break room. She spotted Muldoon, "I hear you might be leaving us Larry." News traveled fast.

"For the most segregated city in America." Trevayne remarked.

"I thought we were." Vicki said sounding almost disappointed.

"Where did you hear that?" Trevayne asked.

"That's all you ever hear."

Looking over at Muldoon he said, "See how it works."

Muldoon was too busy looking at the luscious Vicki Higgins to pay much attention to Trevayne. Vicki Higgins was 25 years old, single and lived with a guy she always referred to as Robert. Marriage was not one of her goals, as she seemed to be more interested in shopping for clothes, dressing nice and being able to party. She had natural blue eyes, soft blonde hair, natural creamy complexion and the nicest smile and sweetest smell of any woman in the office.

She worked in the claims department. No one knew exactly what she did, but she was always on time, seldom called in sick and wasn't the pushy type. The perfect employee.

"Ever been to Omaha?" Muldoon asked her.

"Robert and I went to their zoo once."

"See any blacks there?" Trevayne asked while getting up to leave.

"Wasn't looking for any."

Trevayne smiled at her and carried his coffee to his desk.

"Why is he always pushing that black shit?" She asked Muldoon after he was gone.

"Just how he is. It doesn't bother anyone and I don't think anyone really pays much attention to him. Kind of CMI's Jesse Jackson."

"Well he should put a sock in it all the same. Gets old after awhile."

Muldoon had to agree but then he liked Robinson. He and Trevayne worked well together and he never brought that black shit up when a job had to be done.

"So how are you and Bob?" Muldoon asked.

"Why can't you call him Robert?" She said while taking a seat across from Muldoon. "You know that's his name."

"Most Robert's are called Bob."

"Well he fucks better when he is called Robert." She had a way of saying what she thought didn't have any hang-ups.

Muldoon loved talking to Vicki. He could say things to her he couldn't say to any other woman. She wasn't a paranoid feminist like Wanda, the dip in charge of clerical. All you had to do was look at Wanda crossed eyed, which was the best way to look at her, and she was on the phone to a lawyer talking harassment.

Vicki took a sip from her cup, "so do you think you'll go to Omaha?"

"Want to come along. We could go together." He gave her a knowing wink.

She rolled her eyes to the ceiling. She liked Muldoon, as he was the only guy in the office who was up front with her. She knew that she had a certain sexuality that attracted the men in the office, after all she wasn't born yesterday, but they would make snide remarks behind her back, but Muldoon said them to her and he never made them sound snide.

She didn't know how it got started. She knew that many women would construe what Muldoon said as sexual harassment, especially Wanda the dip in charge of clerical, but Vicki liked sex, and there was nothing wrong with a little flirting. She, at times even thought she'd like doing it with Muldoon, and though she might not be the sharpest knife in the drawer she wasn't a moron. She liked Robert as he paid the bills that gave her the money to buy nice clothes, and she had also met Muldoon's wife, Sarah, and liked her as well. She wouldn't want to hurt someone she liked. She knew where her bread was buttered. And she knew Muldoon was more bluster than anything else.

"If you were married to someone like me you would never get out of bed."

"Why, something wrong with the floor?"

He often wondered where she was when he was 25. He asked her that once and she said, fifth grade.

"You know, Larry, I bet you're a straight lay."

She was right. "What makes you say that?"

"There are some things a woman can sense."

He looked at her and felt it was time to change the subject. "Other than their zoo you know anything about Omaha?"

"They play the College World Series there."

Muldoon thought that that leaves the other fifty weeks open.

"Well I should do some work," she said getting up to leave. "My industrious boss, the Reverend John Bosco has been whining about one thing or another all morning and nothing is getting done."

"You shouldn't call him Reverend."

"Hey the goof was a priest, quit to get married then got divorced and now wants to be a priest again. Talk about an idiot. Anyway that is what Tucker calls him," she said as she left the room.

Muldoon sat alone in the break room wondering what type of Branch Manager they had in Omaha. Muldoon knew his name, John Smith. This is supposedly one of the world's most common names yet this is the only John Smith that Muldoon had ever come across. That was all Muldoon knew about him though, never had a reason to talk to him. He didn't want to move to Omaha and then find out the guy was a jerk. He already worked for a jerk. He sure as hell didn't want to disrupt his family life to work for another one. But then again if he moved the office might have a going away party for him and he might get to kiss Vicki goodbye. That sounded like fun.

"You got a minute Larry?"

He looked somewhat startled. It was Doris Simpson, "sure what is it?"

"Have you seen the Jensen file?"

"Tucker has it."

A look of alarm crossed her face, "what is he doing with it?"

"I gave it to him."

"Jesus tell me you didn't say that."

Muldoon suddenly felt bad for giving the file to Tucker. He didn't know what Doris wanted it for but he knew her concern was genuine. "He asked for it so I gave it to him."

He didn't like his own answer but that is what happened. Usually when Tucker asked for a file the underwriters would stall and check with each other before turning it over to Tucker. They knew that with many prospective risks that it was not good go give Tucker any information that he could use to screw things up. And any information was generally information Tucker could use to screw things up. Tucker did everything by the book; though he never read the book, didn't understand the book and didn't know where the book was he would do anything in his power to make himself look good to the powers that be. Powers that be like everything done by the book as they are basically too stupid to think for themselves. There were occasions when the book had to be ignored. There were certain risks that just didn't fit the book and exceptions would have to be made. This was a part of what underwriting was about, judging a risk by what it is and will be not what some book says it is. You could make a risk acceptable in several ways, adjust the premium, set up a loss control program, bend some rules to make it work, sweet talk, whatever it took. Tucker didn't believe in any of that shit. He felt it was either good or bad, no gray area. Now Muldoon felt bad that he had let Doris down, as he did not check with anyone prior to giving the file to Tucker.

"You didn't check with anyone?" She said sitting down across the table from Muldoon

"No Doris, I'm sorry. Is there a problem with it?

"No, but there will be if he has it."

"Well the only good thing I can tell you is that this morning he was over by me looking for it."

"You mean he may have lost it," she said sounding encouraged.

"With Tucker anything is possible."

"You know Larry we got to write that."

The Jensen file as it became to be known was a chain of bowing alleys that were owned by a Fred Jensen. He owned a couple of fast food franchises in the city as well as a chain of sports bars known as Fast Freddy's. The guy reeked of money. Everything he touched turned to gold. The bowling alleys became available, as people weren't bowling like they use to. They would go to health clubs and exercise and drink mineral water instead of bowling, smoking and drinking beer. Jensen figured with his touch he could get people back into the bowing and make them profitable. Many thought that Jensen was involved with the mob, especially the newspapers who felt anyone that was successful was involved with the mob, which is why most newspapers are not successful, no mob connections. One of Jensen's current insurance companies would not offer him favorable rates on the bowling establishments, which is why CMI was looking at it.

"Don't worry," Muldoon said, "things will work out with it." He got up from the table to refill his cup, "would you like a cup?" He asked her

"Sure, cream and sugar if any."

Muldoon handed her the coffee and asked, "Know anything about Omaha?"

"Other than you being offered the job and having a nice zoo, not much."

"I thought it might be you who would get it."

"No, I don't think Tucker trusts me."

Doris had been with CMI for 11 years. She had come to them from an insurance agency. She was the same age as Muldoon, single and rather plain looking. She used very little make up and had short choppy brown hair and very little make up. She dressed plainly and always looked as if she meant business. No one knew anything about her personal life, other than she was single and lived in an apartment on the near north side. She rarely attended office functions, such as the summer picnic, the office Christmas party, nor would she join in when some of the underwriters would go out for a drink or lunch. She stayed to herself and did her job very well. She had the discipline and the knowledge to make a good underwriting manager. Some thought her to be a lesbian, but she had a sense of humor and wasn't always whining, which more or less eliminated that possibility.

"Why do you think he doesn't trust you?"

"For one thing I rarely understand anything he is talking about and he knows it. One minute he says one thing, the next he contradicts himself. Then when you mention the contradiction he says he wasn't listening. The guy confuses the hell out of me the way he will ask an asinine question and make stupid statements and I can't help but show my bewilderment. And I think he thinks my bewilderment is a fault I shouldn't have."

"If you didn't become bewildered after talking to him that would be the fault." Muldoon said. "That is why he is a branch manager and we aren't."

She took a drink, "you know yesterday I went to see him and he was on the phone. So I thought I would wait a couple of minutes till he got off. Well he never got off, and all the time he was on the phone he never spoke. You figure that out?'

"What was he doing?"

"He was playing with an ear and staring out the window."

"That's it."

"I swear to god Larry that is all he did."

"How long did you wait?"

"Five minutes maybe more."

"Someone could have put him on hold."

"I thought of that so I asked Emma, his secretary, who he was talking to and she said no one."

"So I asked 'why is he on the phone'? And she told me he always spends part of his day on the phone. I think the guy is starting to crack."

"Your best bet is just to ignore him, that's what I do. Do your job and forget him."

"I don't know how you can tune him out like that. There are some things *we do* that he should be aware of."

"Go through Bernie."

"Bernie's retarded." She made a good point.

"Well according to Tucker," Muldoon said, "Bernie is too stupid to be demoted but from what I understand if he becomes really dumb he can get promoted to home office."

"Well," Doris said, "you might be the lucky one getting to get out of here to go to Omaha."

"Would you go if you were me?"

"What does your wife think?"

"She's not sure." Muldoon and his wife talked it over but no decision had been reached. Sarah thought it would be exciting to move but only if things went smooth, but she doubted if things would go smooth. She figured she would spend a lot of time in Omaha lost, not knowing where to buy bread and milk, or how do you find a doctor or a dentist. It sounded exciting but they were going to have to talk some more about it. And then there was the problem of her parents. Sarah was an only child and they felt they must protect her from the evils of the world. They spent the first 10 years of her marriage to Muldoon telling her to keep an eye on him. Sarah never knew what that meant, and when she told Larry he didn't really know either. He simply figured her parents were simply paranoid about their little girl. Her parents were to be over tonight and at that time they would mention the possibility of moving to them. Mentioning it to them probably wasn't a good idea, but as goofy as they were sometimes they would say something that made sense.

"I guess things are different if you're married," Doris said. "If it was me I'd probably go. You got to put some adventure in your life, but I suppose it is easier for a single person to pack up and go. When does Tucker expect an answer?"

"As usual he never really said."

"If I were you I'd just tell him you were seriously thinking about it but you were thinking of taking a drive up there to look around."

"You're very practical," Muldoon told her. He was tempted to ask her why she never married. She was the type of woman that would grow on you. She didn't knock you out with her looks, charm or wit, but she had something.

She finished her coffee and returned to work. Muldoon watched her walk away. He enjoyed talking with her. She was a nice woman. He didn't understand why some guy hadn't hit on her. There were a lot of dippy women in the world married, who didn't have half the brains Doris had, and some didn't even look as good. Yet they were married and Doris wasn't. Life, at times, was hard to figure.

He threw his cup in the garbage and walked back to his cubicle. There was a note saying Tucker wanted to see him

He didn't want to see him now, maybe tomorrow.

THREE

Sarah was sitting at the kitchen table drinking a cup of warm coffee. She was wearing her standard stay at home outfit, faded jeans and an oversized sweatshirt, her hair was pulled back into a ponytail. Larry wasn't home from work and the kids were upstairs doing their homework. She loved the Fall not so much for the change in colors but it meant the start of another school year and peace and quiet from 8-3:30, five days a week.

She had recently signed a petition that some radical group was passing around to get the school year extended to 12 months. She thought this was a great idea, so she signed right up. She knew it wouldn't pass but at the same time she figured there was nothing lost in giving it a shot, and she was at her wit's end, and did admit to it. The start of the school year was welcome relief for all.

The petitioners unfortunately did not gather enough names as the kids in the neighborhood found out about it and simply hounded the poor people as they went door to door. Eventually drove them off.

Sarah was working on her balance sheet. It was blank. She was going to list the advantages and disadvantages of moving on the balance sheet. She had obtained this idea from Oprah or maybe it was Dr. Phil so she decided to give it a shot.

Staring at the blank sheet all she could think of were questions and she didn't know if they should be listed under the plus or the minus side. Finally she decided the hell with it and wrote down her questions on a separate piece or paper and headed it *Questions.* She numbered them.

1. Will we be able to sell the house?

2. Will we be able to find a new one?

3. Will we be able to get a mortgage?

4. Who will move us?

5. Will the movers look like they should be the subject of a daytime talk show?

6. What are the schools like?

7. Will the kids miss their friends and become lonesome?

8. Will they be able to make new friends?

9. Will I spend most of her time lost not knowing where anything is?

10. Will we be happier there than here?

11. What about our parents?

She stopped writing. The list was starting to look like something Martha Stewart would write. She wondered if Dr. Phil and Oprah approve of Martha. Does she approve of them? That could be a list.

The list was way too long and she knew that there would be no trouble with Larry's parents, or with his family. His parents were retired and lived in Florida and only came north at Thanksgiving and would stay thru Christmas, and they didn't care what any of their children did as long as they didn't have to pay for it.

Larry's older brother was a priest in Rome, and he would tell them he would keep them in his prayers. Larry's sister lived in Columbus with her husband and 4 children and she would tell them that if they could do it so could Sarah and Larry. His younger brother was a minor league umpire in California and couldn't care less in what they did. The more she thought of Larry's family the more she thought why they should care. All of them, with the exception of Larry had already flown the coop.

She then thought of her parents. A frown crossed her face. She walked over to the coffeepot and refilled her cup. She returned to the table thinking of the grief they could cause.

Sarah was an only child, and her parents were *only parents.* Sarah was 35, married for 13 years, mother of three children, held a part time job, dabbled in poetry, and the keeper of the house and yet her parents babied her. Or perhaps it was only concern they were showing.

Larry had told her that her parents were paranoid. She didn't know what would be worse, moving to another state, or telling her parents they were moving to another state. They just never seemed to understand. It took them almost 12 years to accept Larry and there were times that acceptance was rather dubious.

When she and Larry would get together with his family on Thanksgiving there would be food, fun, drink and laughter. Then they would get together with her parents on Christmas and have the same conversation they have had every Christmas she could remember since they were married. The kids would show their grandparents the gifts they had received and one grandparent would say, "You're spending too much money on these gifts. You should save your money."

Then last Christmas Larry told her parents that they were thinking of going to Disney World, and stay with his parents while there. His parents lived in Sebring about 2 hours from Disney World. She knew he said it just to aggravate them, though they had talked about going they had yet to do so, but her parents told them it was too much money to spend for a vacation and that there were a lot of bugs in Florida. Larry then told them he liked bugs and that Emily, their daughter, was thinking of becoming an entomologist. They turned white with fear that an 11 year old girl would want to be an entomologist. But as if on cue Emily said she did, though she didn't know what an entomologist was it sounded like it could be fun. Then after dinner her mother got her alone in the kitchen and told her that Larry was undermining the children. It made her angry to think her mother would say that about Larry, but when she told Larry he only smiled and told her they were paranoid. She was beginning to think he might be right.

She decided to stop thinking about her parents, as it was depressing her, and anyway they would be over tonight. They made a point of dropping in at least once a week, and it was usually

Monday as there was never anything any good on TV on Monday. She didn't know if this was true or not as she had never gotten to see any TV on Monday.

With the kids back in school and her days now free. Her part time job was 3 evenings a week and Saturday morning at a local grocery store; she made a vow that she would spend some time each day working on her poetry. Her poetry was simply that, *her poetry*. She had been writing it on and off for several years. She had even entered a poetry contest and though she didn't win she did receive *Honorable Mention*, which is the politically correct way of saying you *lost*. It use to bother her, but not anymore. She felt the writing was good therapy for her. She loved every part of it, the writing, the editing, the re-writing, more editing. She thought it helped to keep her normal.

She had neighbors, who had a life style similar to her own, but they were on Valium and couple smoked dope and one was in therapy and she knew of one that was having an affair. They told her they did these things because they were tense. She found writing eliminated any tenseness she may have had. It didn't keep her awake at night, and she found the time she was writing would fly by. Larry told her to go for it.

At first she was embarrassed by her poems. Eventually she worked up the nerve to show some to him. He was surprised that she wrote, but he read them and found them to be as good as any poetry he had read. There were now times, at night, after the kids had gone to bed that she would show Larry some of her work and ask for his suggestions. He would never try to interfere, but he would on occasion have something useful to say about what she had written and she would use it. She could tell just by watching his face as he read if she was on the right track that brought her encouragement. She was going to complete a book of poetry. She didn't know when but she knew she could do it, and who knew, maybe she could get it published. They had a nice life. It was simple, but nice. She wondered if it would be this nice in Omaha.

She looked down at the list of questions she had written and shrugged. She took the list and placed it in the kitchen drawer. She heard him pull into the driveway.

"What time are your parents getting here?" he asked while giving her a kiss.

"I told them about six thirty. So you have about half an hour to get ready."

"I told the boys they could watch some of Monday Night Football if they got their homework done."

"They're doing it now."

The twins, Timmy and Terry would always get their homework done early on Monday night to watch football. Though they never made it to the end of a game due to all the commercials, TV time outs, and listening to lame commentary. It was usually bedtime before half time. Muldoon would tell them they should thank their lucky stars they don't live on the East Coast or they would never see an entire Monday Night game in their lifetime.

The doorbell rang. They were early. Larry looked and Sarah, gave her another quick kiss said, "Hang in there."

"I haven't even changed," she said taking off up the stairs to do so.

Muldoon was going to have to face them alone.

"Hi Larry," Sarah's mother Joyce said giving him a hug. She was a short stout lady with gentle features. She had the look of a grandmother but not the temperament of one. It was only in the past six months that she started hugging him. Larry didn't know what brought it on but it was now her standard method of greeting. "And how is my little girl?" She said spying Emily coming in to the room.

Sarah's father Hal simply said hi and walked in.

The twins then came bounding into the room. Hal stepped back as these two frightened him. A couple of years ago they filled the back of his pick up truck with water simply to see if it leaked. It was like filling a swimming pool. When Hal saw this he went running out into the street yelling, "What the hell are you doing?"

"Filling the back of your truck with water."

Not thinking he opened the tailgate and damn near got washed a way. Knocked him down and he got soaked. By some miracle he didn't get hurt, but ever since that day he was leery of *the boys* as he referred to them.

"We are going to watch Monday Night Football tonight Grandpa," he was informed.

"Don't you have homework?" Joyce asked.

Just then Sarah came in and greeted her parents with hugs. Joyce was always happy to see her daughter and gave her a big smile and a hug. Larry got everyone a drink, Manhattans, except for Sarah who drank wine. Small talk was made and Larry sensed that Sarah wanted to wait till after dinner to break the news about Omaha. Sarah suggested a second drink before dinner and Larry assumed she wanted them somewhat relaxed or in the bag when the news was delivered.

The boys ate quickly and efficiently and when finished were given permission to go watch all the pre-game bullshit on ESPN.

Emily decided it would be a good time to take a bath. At times she was smart beyond her years.

Coffee was served. Sarah cleared her throat and took a deep breath. "We have some news," she started, "we may be moving to Omaha."

Silence followed by silence.

It lasted seconds but seemed like an hour. Larry looked at Sarah, and their eyes locked briefly. He looked at his watch then the clock. He looked at his mother in law, she hadn't blinked, a blank stare. Hal just sat there looking distinguished. Hal was 65 looked 10 years younger, had snow white hair, always looked as if he just walked in from outside. Muldoon saw his eyebrows move up slightly, but that was the only sign of life.

Then Hal spoke, "I think Marlin Perkins was in Omaha. He had a TV show *Wild Kingdom* I think it was called. He was always wrestling something. He had an assistant that was always off in the bush or wherever while Marlin was wrestling something. Saw him wrestle an Anaconda once and it damn near stopped my heart as I thought for sure Marlin was a goner.

"He was in Chicago at one time too." Hal continued suddenly full of information. "Had a show here called *Zoo Parade* or some such. Never wrestled anything but did get bit a lot by snakes as I recall. Quite an interesting guy."

This wasn't the answer Muldoon was expecting. And he thought he would like to see that anaconda adventure, as it seemed to be the highlight of Marlin's career.

Sarah too was somewhat perplexed just vaguely remembering Marlin.

Joyce blinked and said, "Good god, Omaha."

"Is this a promotion?"

Larry looked over at his father in law and didn't exactly know what to tell him. The more he thought the more he wasn't sure if he even had the job. Was he putting the cart ahead of the horse?

Before he could answer Hal said, "Well you got to go where the money is."

"Omaha? Joyce said.

"I think more people live in Chicago than in the entire state of Nebraska."

The only thing Muldoon could figure was that the Manhattans had gotten to Hal. He was making sense when he wasn't making sense.

"Where is Omaha?" Joyce asked.

"Just the other side of Iowa," Hal told her. Then as if he had a brainstorm he shouted, "Omaha Steaks!"

Everyone turned and looked at Hal. "Omaha Steaks come from Omaha, but I have never had one." Then he thought for a moment and said, "Well maybe they come from Nebraska but only use Omaha in their name."

Was he done Muldoon wondered. He looked at Sarah. Sarah too was perplexed by her dad. Under normal circumstances he would have all kinds of questions or concerns about this move. But it didn't seem to have any affect at all other than some off the wall comments.

"Will you be home for Christmas?" Joyce wanted to know.

"I doubt if we will have even moved by Christmas." Larry told her. He had not even thought of a timetable. He and Sarah thought they would make a trip out to Omaha, look it over. Get an idea on home prices and schools, and stores and simply see what kind of town it was. He doubted if CMI could do anything in three months or less. But then it did take them only about three minutes to can 15% of their work force. So anything may be possible.

"What are we going to do when you are gone?" Here it comes Muldoon thought. Joyce will be a victim of some type in all of this.

Muldoon wanted to tell her that why not just go on with your lives but he thought better of it, "you will always be welcome to come and visit."

"Winter driving can be bad."

"You could always fly." Sarah suggested.

"And put up with all that searching of your luggage. I hear they even search people's shoes."

"The only thing I ever put in my shoes have been my feet." Hal said

Muldoon was slowly loosing interest in this conversation. After all he wasn't really sure if he had this promotion. And he knew little, if anything about Omaha. There could be the chance he and Sarah might not like the city. Or maybe the job simply isn't cracked up to be what he thinks he might be. Maybe he should be like Trevayne Robinson and simply go with the flow and hope to survive to a nice quiet, secure retirement.

Timmy came into the room, "the Packers are up twenty one zip."

"That is because they have a quarterback." Hal told them

"You and your brother should start getting ready for bed. Tomorrow is still a school day." Sarah told him.

He frowned but went to get his brother and get ready for bed.

Muldoon watched him walk away and wondered how would all this affect his kids? He and Sarah were lucky. Their kids were good, of course everyone thinks their kids are good, but Sarah and he had little trouble with them. Though at times Timmy and Terry could be adventuresome but no real problems. And Emily was simply a nice girl. Would they be able to adjust to Omaha? How much input should they have? Muldoon decided he was thinking too much. "Anyone like an after dinner drink?"

"Sure," Hal answered before the question barely had left Muldoon's mouth.

The remainder of the evening was quiet. Joyce seemed to be somewhat dumbfounded about the possible move. Wondering if she would ever see her grand children again. Hal seemed not to care.

After all had left and Sarah and Larry were in bed Larry said, "That was kind of a strange evening. Your mother worrying about seeing here grandkids and your dad like he didn't care."

"You never know what people are going to do."

Muldoon found that to be true. No matter how you thought someone was gong to react it never seemed to work out that way.

He leaned over to kiss her goodnight, "who is Marlin Perkins?" She wanted to know.

He shrugged, "some zoo guy they all grew up with I think."

FOUR

Muldoon stood in the doorway to Joe Tucker's office; Tucker appeared to be on the phone. He was turned in his chair facing the rear window. Muldoon could see the start of a bald spot on the back of Tucker's head. Muldoon waited a moment, Tucker turned and saw Muldoon and with a startled expression hung up the phone.

Muldoon found this strange but just about everything about Joe Tucker was strange. "You want to see me, "Muldoon said.

"I do?" Tucker had already forgotten the note he left for Muldoon yesterday.

Muldoon could sense that whatever it was Tucker wanted to see him about was not going to surface immediately. "There was a note on my desk saying you did."

"Oh yeah," Tucker said suddenly remembering, "Come on in, have a seat," he pointed to the two chairs that faced his desk.

Muldoon entered the office. Tucker and the Claims Manager were the only two people that had their own offices. Everyone else was stuck with a cubicle. Tucker's office was a palace compared to the rest of the office. He had a large solid oak desk, high back, leather, swivel chair, and an oak cadenza behind his desk. There were several pictures on the wall depicting the outdoor life though Tucker was what one would call an in door man.

The office was located in a corner which gave Tucker a view that while not breathtaking was exciting. From his windows he could see the hustle on the streets below, occasionally hear the traffic and check out the other offices and people with binoculars he kept in his top desk drawer. If he looked long and hard enough and it was a clear day you could see the lake. The windows extended from two feet above the floor to the ceiling. The office made Tucker look important which was exactly CMI's intent. All their manager offices were made to look as if the man occupying them was in charge. Even if the man occupying them was a flunky as was pretty much the case with Joe Tucker.

Muldoon took a seat. Tucker was wearing a new blue pin striped business suit, a crisp white shirt and solid maroon tie. He may not be smart but he knew how to dress smart. If nothing else it made him look like a Branch Manager.

"Well what can I do for you Larry?"

"You wanted to see me, remember?"

"Not really, but if you say so I will."

There then was 30 seconds of silence. Tucker sat in his large high back, leather swivel chair with his hands folded over his stomach as if in deep thought. Muldoon watched him not really knowing what was going on. Tucker closed his eyes and started to roll back and forth in the chair. Muldoon watched him rock. It appeared that Tucker was starting to pick up speed. The chair started sliding towards the window at the right rear of his desk. Muldoon started to become alarmed, "is there something wrong," he blurted out.

Tucker stopped rocking, opened his eyes and smiled, "No, only remembering."

"Remembering what?"

"Trying to remember what I wanted to see you about. You sure it was you I wanted to see?'

"That is what the note said."

"Ah the note, physical evidence that I wanted to see you." Tucker rubbed his hands together, "now we are getting somewhere."

Muldoon wanted to scream and call him one big stupid fucking idiot but he doubted if Tucker would understand anything so basic.

Tucker spoke, "how are things in Omaha?"

"I haven't gone *yet*."

"So then you're going?" Tucker smiled. He was happy to hear that Muldoon would be leaving.

"I haven't decided if I'm going to Omaha."

"Oh," Tucker sounded concerned, "Don't you like the zoo?"

"Never seen it."

"You know," Tucker said leaning forward on his desk, "everyone says they have a nice zoo but I don't know anyone who has seen it. How can it be a nice zoo if no one has seen it?"

Muldoon wasn't going to get involved. "Is there anything specific you wanted to see me about as I do have work to do."

"You're the only one. That Vicki Higgins hasn't done a damn thing all day except drink coffee. She is damn lucky she is good looking. And her boss, the Reverend Bosco, is in his usual daze. All he seems to do is watch her drink coffee and play with himself."

Tucker did not understand the Claims Manager, John Bosco. Bosco the married ex-priest who was now in the process of becoming a divorced ex-priest. This boggled Tucker's mind that a man would leave the priesthood to get married and then want to get divorced. It boggled most married men that anyone would want to leave the priesthood to get married. They obviously didn't know when they had it made. Tucker considered himself to be a devout Catholic, but this was by Tucker's standards not the Church's.

"Did you know," Tucker said as if passing on a big secret to Muldoon, "that Father Bosco is getting divorced?"

"I don't think it is necessary to call him Father."

"Once a priest always a priest." Tucker exclaimed. "I bet the poor man's mother is rolling over in her grave knowing that her son is doing what he is doing, which brings us to the Jensen file."

Muldoon was temporarily caught off guard by the way Tucker worked the Jensen file into the conversation, "It does?" Muldoon asked.

"Definitely," Tucker answered. He reached for a pile of papers that were located on the cadenza behind him and picked up what Muldoon could only assume was the Jensen file. "See this," Tucker said waving it in the air.

Muldoon nodded.

"Did you know that Jensen is a mobster?"

"Never been proved."

"*The Chicago Tribune* thinks he's a mobster."

"No. They only accuse him of being a Democrat and contributing to Democratic causes."

"What the hell's the difference?" Tucker said in a raised voice. "And now we want to insure his goddam bowling alleys?"

"It's a good risk."

"Why?"

Muldoon didn't feel up to getting into all the details as insurance was not a subject that Tucker always understood, of course neither did Muldoon or anyone with normal intelligence for that matter, but he felt he owed it to Doris, "Well," Muldoon began.

Tucker interrupted, "would he by chance have any gay bars in these bowling alleys, or maybe perhaps sponsor some gay bowlers?" Never hurts to ask Tucker thought to himself.

Muldoon didn't know where Tucker was leading but he answered, "I think he does."

"Does what? Bars or bowlers?

"Both." Muldoon said.

"And a Democrat to boot. What a cross the man must bear. Would you by chance know if knows anything about lobes?"

"About what?"

"Lobes."

"Lobes?"

"Lobes."

"What's a lobe?"

"That's not important." Tucker said, as he didn't want the whole office to know his secret of sucking up to the bosses. "Perhaps there is more to this than meets the eye," he handed the file to Muldoon. "Give this to Simpson and tell her she did a good job."

Muldoon took the file, "so we're going to write it?"

"Of course. This Jensen sounds queerer than a three-dollar bill. Why the hell wouldn't we write it?"

"Those were my thoughts as well," Muldoon agreed. Muldoon was starting to wish he was working at the Omaha Zoo instead of the one CMI had here in Chicago as he had no ideal on why being queer had anything to do with the file.

"Now," Tucker said leaning back in his chair, "how are things coming along with that town with the zoo?"

"Omaha?"

"That's the place. You decide anything yet."

"No, my wife and I are still discussing it.'

"You talk things over with your wife, Jesus H. Christ."
Tucker sounded alarmed.

"Yes."

"Why?"

"Because she's my wife."

"That the only reason."

"There are others but that is the main one."

"Well to each his own. What does the wife say?"

"Well we haven't really decided anything yet?"

"So what do you talk about?"

"When?"

"When you talk about going to Omaha."

"Whether we should go or not."

"Well of course you should go, so what's the problem?"

"There's no problem."

"Then you'll be going."

"Only after we decide."

"Decide what?"

"Decide if we want to go."

"Why wouldn't you want to go?

"We haven't decided."

"Are you trying to confuse me Larry?

"No."

"Good, now where were we?"

"Is this job official?" Muldoon asked hoping to get a specific answer but doubted seriously if he would.

"What job?"

"The job in Omaha."

"Of course or almost of course. I have a call into Schwartz now at the Home Office recommending you. Just a matter of him getting back to me. You know how those Home Office people never return phone calls, the dumb fucks. But Larry between you and me it is yours." Tucker had no way of knowing if this was true or not, but he could not imagine CMI not wanting Muldoon moving up the old corporate ladder. Young, bright, stable home life. A perfect choice.

Muldoon let it slide. He knew Schwartz. Schwartz was a Home Office flunky but from dealings Muldoon had with him in the past almost normal for a Home Office flunky. Schwartz, for a Home Office flunky, had a somewhat positive outlook on life. Muldoon was starting to feel better about the job offer.

"You see Roundtree?" Muldoon asked. Muldoon wanted to change the subject and get off of Omaha and since Roundtree went storming out of the office yesterday Muldoon hadn't seen him.

"Who is Roundtree?"

"The guy in the cubicle next to mine."

"You mean the Indian?"

"I don't know his nationality."

"Well he is an Indian. What did you think; with a name like Roundtree he was going to be Italian?" Tucker was the type of person where he heard a name, he would try to place that person, by nationality, religion or a combination thereof.

"Well I was just wondering where he was." Muldoon said wondering why he even brought it up.

"Heard he needed some time with his kid. Whatever the hell that means."

Every conversation that Muldoon had with Tucker seemed to wander aimlessly about. The man was an absolute riddle. How things ever got done at all surprised Muldoon. Muldoon wanted to end this conversation but he just couldn't get up and walk out. As much of a fool he thought Tucker was, he did deserve some respect, if only for the title he held.

"Talking about my promotion." Muldoon said trying to make it sound as an after thought.

"I thought we were talking about Roundtree."

"Well I just want to be sure it is pretty much official."

"So what are your thoughts again?" Tucker said as if he never heard the question and probably didn't.

"Like you said we're going to think it over and probably take a drive there and look around."

"Sounds often damn reasonable to me. You sure I said that?"

"Yeah."

"Well if you must, talk it over with the wife, family and friends." Tucker hesitated. "You still have those twin boys?"

"Yeah."

"You going to bring them with you?"

"If we go we will."

"You're a brave man Larry."

A few years ago CMI had a picnic for employees and families. The twins let the air out of the tires of all the cars there.

Quite the adventure. That is one thing Tucker never forgot or anyone else in the office for that matter. Most look back on it now and laugh, except for Tucker. Of course at the time no one laughed. Both Sarah and Larry were quite embarrassed, but fortunately time does heal some wounds.

"What are their names again?"

"Terry and Timmy."

"Oh yeah, TNT. Well I'm sure they'll like Omaha, got a lot of tires up there filled with air I'm told. They could probably have a lot of fun in the zoo parking lot." Tucker let out a smile.

"I'm sure they could." Muldoon agreed

"Well okay, we'll talk more about it Saturday."

"I don't come in on Saturday."

"Oh yeah," Tucker said, "I forgot, you're somewhat normal. Then let's make it Friday on company time."

Muldoon dropped off the Jensen file on Doris's desk. She was not there. He thought of walking over to Vicki's cubicle but decided not to. He thought his time would be better spent giving John Smith in Omaha a call. He entered his cubicle and there waiting for him was John Bosco

"Oh hi Larry," Bosco said, "you got a minute?"

"I suppose." Muldoon walked behind his desk and sat down. "What do you need?"

Bosco sat across from Muldoon and started to fidget. Muldoon watched as Bosco was obviously working up his nerve to ask Muldoon something.

Bosco was an olive skinned Italian with very little hair. Muldoon figured it was god's revenge. Muldoon found it ironic that when a woman became a nun some had their hair cut short and when they came out of the convent they wanted a full head of hair. Whereas priests went into the priesthood with a full head of hair and when they came out they hardly had any.

John Bosco was a bald ex-priest who chewed his nails. He left the priesthood six years ago to get married. He had been a priest for seven years when he met a young lady named Sheila Gray. He was struck by her immediately and she by him. He knew that priests would always have normal urges but the urge he had for Sheila Gray was overpowering. She was the fifth grade teacher in their parish school, and had a body that wouldn't quit.

One afternoon after school, John Bosco was in the school gym shooting some baskets. It was his form of exercise. That day she had decided to take a short cut through the gym to her car in the parking lot when their eyes met. It was only her third day on the job and she didn't know he was a priest, and he didn't know she was a teacher. Their eyes met and immediately locked.

John Bosco walked over to her while dribbling the basketball all the while trying to look athletic and commanding. She watched in amusement and fascination. He introduced himself and made no mention of the fact that he was a priest. She was so infatuated that she didn't even think of asking him what he was doing in the gym. She never thought that priests would play basketball; she assumed he was a custodian of some type. He never thought of asking her why she was in the gym. He was simply glad she was there.

They made small talk for a few minutes and then he asked her if she would like to out for a drink. His conscience never bothered him, as having a drink with an attractive woman is not a sin. At first she showed some reluctance in accepting his invitation but his dark brown eyes, olive skin and perfectly straight white teeth convinced her to say yes. Plus he still had hair. He asked if she would mind waiting a few minutes while he changed. She told him to take his time. He ducked in the locker room, took a quick shower and changed into a pair of slacks and sports shirt the uniform priests wear when they are not on the prowl for lost souls.

It was in the bar that she asked him what his occupation was. He told her. She never flinched. She had never made it with a priest before, but she did that night.

He wasn't very good at it but she felt he had potential. He felt good about it though he knew he wasn't supposed to. They met regularly for the next six months. They would meet occasionally for lunch or in the evening. When there was a school holiday such as a Holy Day of Obligation they would spend the most of the day and part of the evening together. The pastor, Father Wentworth, was never suspicious. He was an old man in a wealthy parish. The grammar school was well attended. The few nuns that were still there ran the school well. The parishioners were generous. There was no parish debt and his assistant Father John Bosco seemed like a nice young priest who always said his mass, preached nice little sermons and was well liked by the parishioners. Even if Father Wentworth knew he wouldn't have said anything as long as the books balanced, and the books always balanced.

The love and passion between John Bosco and Sheila Gray grew until finally she approached him on the subject of marriage. He was prepared for the question and told her if he had to choose between her and God he would pick her, but it might take him some time to get out of his vows. She said she would be willing to wait.

He went to Father Wentworth with his decision to leave the priesthood and Farther Wentworth told him to go to hell. Father Wentworth wondered why a nice young priest like John Bosco, assigned to a nice wealthy parish where the parishioners got baptized, married and then moved to other parishes to die would give it all up for a woman. He then told him to go see the Bishop.

The Bishop told him to go to hell and that if he really wanted to leave the priesthood to go ahead and leave, as fornicating priests would give the church a bad image.

John Bosco felt somewhat guilty about his broken vows but when he told Sheila he was ready to marry her she did things to him the he only fantasized about. The guilty feeling then left him about the same time she finished filling his every fantasy, and some he didn't even know he had.

Soon after that Sheila lost her job. However with the education John Bosco had he had no difficulty in obtaining one. He was hired as a claims adjuster for CMI. Though the man that hired him was drunk he knew he could make it in the outside world.

Three months later they made it official by getting married. Sheila got another teaching job, this time in a suburban public school. They bought a condo and lived happily ever after until about four months ago when John Bosco found out that his wife was making it with the stationary engineer at the Walden School where she taught.

Bosco spoke, "Larry is your brother still a priest?"

"Yeah, why?"

"Is he still in Rome?"

"Yeah."   Muldoon's brother, who was 8 years older than Larry, was in Rome as a teacher of Church Doctrine to seminarians and priests who were on sabbaticals.

"Can he get me an annulment?"

"A what?" Muldoon was somewhat surprised by the request.

"An annulment. I need an annulment."

"I thought you were getting divorced?"

"I am but an annulment would be the frosting on the cake."

Muldoon was somewhat confused. "But if you are getting divorced why do you need an annulment?"

"To get back in the church's good graces."

"How?"

"If I can get my marriage annulled then I can say I was never married, and if I was never married I could never have been divorced and I can get my old job back of being a priest."

Muldoon had thought he had heard it all but obviously not, "I don't think it works like that. Wouldn't it be easier to just get divorced and let it go at that."

"The church does not look favorably on divorced Catholics," Bosco said.

"You mean they look favorably on *annulled* Catholics?" Muldoon asked.

"Sure." Bosco answered confidently. "If you are divorced Catholic it means you were once married and therefore not eligible to receive the sacraments, but if you are annulled Catholic it means the church thinks that there was no marriage and you are as good as new."

"But you were married."

"Not if I get it annulled."

"But divorced Catholics can receive the sacraments as long as they don't remarry."

"Yeah, but what if they want to remarry or go back to being a priest?"

Muldoon didn't know why he was pursuing this conversation as it all sounded like a bunch of mumbo jumbo to him. "Well what do you want me to do?" Muldoon sounded flustered.

"I want to talk to your brother in Rome."

"For what?"

"So he can grease the skids so to speak."

"He can?" Muldoon didn't know exactly what his brother did in Rome other than teach the young seminarians the joy of celibacy, but doubted if he had anything to do with annulments.

Bosco leaned forward in his chair and spoke confidentially, "I'm willing to pay Larry."

Muldoon became interested. He was wondering how far this goof was willing to go, "How much?"

"Two thousand dollars."

Muldoon decided to try and string him along. "The last I heard the going rate was closer to five thousand."

"Five thousand," Bosco yelped, "why that is highway robbery."

"It pays to be good."

"Don't you have any influence with your brother?" Bosco was starting to sound worried. He didn't have five thousand. He could barely scrounge up two and with the divorce settlement looming, he might not even have that.

"Well John," Muldoon said trying to sound as if he knew what he was talking about. "Everybody over there has their hand out. My brother has to get his cut, and then there are others who have to be take care of, to how did you put it, 'to grease the skids', it all adds up."

"But five thousand dollars."

"Well maybe you and Sheila can work out your differences."

"That fornicating floozie," Bosco said. "Why should I work out anything with her?"

"To save five thousand dollars."

"Well I'll have to think about it Larry, that's a lot of money. Is there any chance that you can get them to come down some?

"I doubt it." Muldoon spoke with confidence as it was fun conning this goof. "As you know money talks, and lets face it the more you have the easier it will go for you."

"But five thousand dollars," Bosco didn't know where he would come up with that kind of money. "Why when I was a priest you could get one for under two thousand, even less. Just answer a questionnaire, give them a check then wait forever." And Bosco didn't want to wait forever.

"Inflation is a bitch."

Bosco leaned back in the chair and ran his hand over his bald head, "I'll see what I can do."

"By the way John you know anything about Omaha?"

92

"Sheila and I went to their zoo during our happier days. They do have a nice zoo."

"So I've heard."

"You taking the job?"

"Haven't decided."

"Well if you go lets keep in touch I might be able to raise that money and I would like to know where you are in case I have to get it to you."

Muldoon was convinced the guy was a goof. Willing to spend money to get a marriage annulled, as if you were going to fool God. Out of the corner of his eye Muldoon could see John Tucker heading towards the cubicle.

"Say Larry," Tucker said upon entering the cubicle, "Oh good morning Father," he said when he saw Bosco.

"Good morning." Bosco frowned

"I hope I'm not interrupting anything important," Tucker said.

"You're not." Bosco told him even though Bosco felt what was being discussed was important he did not want Tucker a part of it.

"Then you are wasting company time," Tucker stated matter of factly.

Muldoon knew that he was not going to get involved in this exchange as Tucker could trap you more ways with his absent minded talk.

"I should be going," Bosco said while getting up to leave.

"That would be nice," Tucker said. "Give my regards to the Missus, if she is still around," Tucker said as Bosco left.

They both watched him leave.

"You shouldn't be so hard on him?" Muldoon said.

"Why the hell not?"

"We all make mistakes."

"He already had made two."

"No one's perfect."

"Least of all him."

Muldoon could tell that he wasn't going to change Tucker's dislike for John Bosco so he decided to get at the business at hand, "what can I do for you?"

"When?"

"Now."

"What would you like to do for me?"

If Muldoon had a gun he would have shot him. "I assumed you came by for a purpose."

"I did?" Tucker asked.

"Well why else would you be here?"

"We all have to be someplace, which reminds me," Tucker said as if in mid thought, "what are you doing for lunch tomorrow?"

Muldoon was afraid to answer. Did Tucker want to go out to lunch with him? That would be unbearable. Spending 45 minutes with Tucker would be mind boggling. Muldoon took a glance at his phone hoping it would ring so he could answer it and not answer the question. If he told Tucker had had no plans, which was true, then Tucker might ask him to join him for lunch. If he said he was busy he would then have to find something to do for lunch to avoid having lunch with Tucker. He was in a no win situation. "I don't know," he finally answered.

"Good. How about having lunch with Harry Schmidt?"

"I'm not thirsty." Harry Schmidt was an agent who had the reputation for drinking his lunch. He had tremendous capacity for booze. Usually when an underwriter went out to lunch with Harry he was shot for the rest of the afternoon and the better part of the next day. "Why me?" Muldoon asked, "He is Roundtree's agent."

"Roundtree still hasn't returned. Vicki says he went home to shoot his kid for becoming a lawyer and has yet to return."

"Sounds rather drastic."

"Not really, but he is going to be docked. If he wanted time off he only had to ask. Sounds like he has a legitimate reason."

Tucker left without an answer from Muldoon for that Muldoon was grateful.

Muldoon hit the button on his phone that turned on the voice mail that said, *This is Larry Muldoon I am not able to take your call right now as I am either on the phone or away from my desk. Please leave your name and number and a brief message and I will get back to you as soon as possible. Thanks for calling.*

What a lie. Voice mail was set up for one reason and one reason only. To avoid the phone. Muldoon wanted it quiet as he wanted to do some thinking. He wanted to think about Omaha and moving up the old corporate ladder.

He thought it would be nice to get away from Chicago. Not that he had anything against Chicago, but though he told people he lived there he actually lived in Lombard a western suburb. The only time he went into the city was to go to work and he was pretty sick of the train ride. He got the train in Lombard and it was a straight shot to the Loop it was still a pain. He could not recall the last time he and Sarah actually went into the Loop to do anything.

If they would go out to eat it would be a restaurant near their house, or a movie near their home. Even if they went to a play, which was rare, it would be some dinner theater near their house or in another suburb.

Use to go to baseball games but the cell phone crowd had taken over Wrigley Field and basically ruined it for baseball fans. Plus the parking was a joke. Driving to the south side to see the Sox simply wasn't worth the effort, and baseball seemed to have only one goal and that was to gouge the fan as often as possible. Like the World Series was on now and there wasn't even an office pool.

The Bears sucked. No quarterback and the chances were they would not have one before the next Millennium if then. And for whatever reason tickets to Bear games were hard to come by, unless you wanted to pay through the nose to see a team without a quarterback.

Muldoon figured that if they moved to Omaha they would probably do more in Omaha then they now do in Chicago. Plus it would be a promotion, more money. He got out the company directory and looked up information on the Omaha Office. It handled Nebraska, North and South Dakota, Kansas, Colorado, Idaho, Montana. He would be Underwriting Manager for seven states. Of course no one actually lived in those states, probably more people in Cook County than all those states combined, but it would still be added responsibility.

More responsibility, more money perhaps even more prestige, if that meant anything. He and Sarah would truly be off on their own. Not that they weren't now but somehow it seemed moving to Nebraska would somehow make it official.

The more Muldoon thought about it the more he wanted the challenge. He knew he could handle the job and all that went with it. Moving the kids might be difficult but not something that could not be overcome. Their kids were pretty well adjusted and he didn't really see any problem there.

He thought of Sarah being off in a strange town by herself and felt it would probably be harder for her than anyone else. But they would always have each other, and Sarah wasn't dumb. She could rise to most any occasion and usually did.

He would wait to hear to what Schwartz had to say, but he could not think of any reason why he should not go.

Then he heard it. He stood up in his cubicle and looked over at the wall clock. He saw that it was almost three. About the half the office was over looking their cubicles then checking their watches.

Phillips was right on schedule. Nothing like a good nap to help the day go faster.

FIVE

Sarah thought it was a good poem, *Loveliness is Loneliness and Loneliness is Love* She had been working on it for about a week and now was ready to submit it. One of these days she would win one of these contests. She just had to find the address on where to send it and she would be on her way.

The address was hid somewhere on her computer and it was just a matter of time of tracking it down, finding the correct file when the phone rang.

"What are you doing?" It was her friend Nancy who spoke before Sarah could even give a greeting. Nancy lived across the street and had arrived from Detroit about the same time she and Larry moved in. They became best of friends instantly. It is one of those things that happen every now and then. You meet someone and instantly there is a connection.

"Not much."

"You want to *do lunch* as they say in Hollywood?"

Sarah thought about it for about a second or two and thought why not? It would give her chance to talk to someone about the move to Omaha. Nancy, after all, had moved here from Detroit and seemed to have adjusted quite well

"Where do you want to go?" Sarah asked.

"How about that little la de da place with the queer waiters over near Woodfield I'll drive. And if some reason they are not working we can always shop."

Sarah knew the place but she wasn't sure the waiters were queer. Nancy thought that just about everyone was queer, and if not queer different. It would be enjoyable to spend part of the afternoon with her. As she was fun and always had a nice lookout on life.

"I will pick you up at 11:30.

* * *

Muldoon found Schmidt sitting in a booth alone along the wall. Schmidt had a German name but an Irish face, and he always looked happy with life. He stood less than six feet tall and weighed a beefy two hundred pounds ,thinning gray hair, rosy cheeks and an opinion or thought on just about anything.

Schmidt owned an insurance agency in the northwest suburbs known as Schmidt and Son though he never had a son. He was twenty-five when he started the business and gave it that name for he thought that people would not deal with a twenty-five year old just starting out. His thought was his customers would see the title and figure he was the son and that there was a more experienced member of the firm at the top making sure things were right. And it worked.

He also figured if all went according to plan someday he would have a son who would take over the business, but instead he was blessed with three daughters none of who were interested in life, health, property or casualty.

Muldoon slid in the booth across from him wondering why Schmidt wanted to meet him for lunch.

They shook hands, "What do you want to drink?" He asked Muldoon

"I'll have iced tea."

Schmidt frowned, "Cripe, I remember when underwriters were allowed to have a drink or two at lunch. Now you people can't take a dump unless it is in an employee manual somewhere." Schmidt looked around for the waitress.

Muldoon smiled. He noticed that Schmidt was having a Manhattan on the rocks, which was Schmidt's idea of not drinking at lunch. If he was seriously drinking he would be having it straight up.

The waitress stopped by and Muldoon gave her his drink order and he reached for a menu. "Joe tells me you wanted to see me and I am kind of curious why as you are not my agent."

Schmidt looked at him, "well my underwriter is off somewhere antagonizing his son. Hear the kid wants to be a lawyer. Roundtree should kill him."

"I think that might be the plan."

"Like this country needs another shit head lawyer." Schmidt was off and running. "You would think any decent law school would simply say. We have enough of these bastards out there. Let's have a moratorium. No more lawyers for five years."

Muldoon's iced tea arrived and he took a sip. He was going to agree with Schmidt's assessment on too many lawyers, but thought better of it. When you had lunch with Schmidt it was he that did most of the drinking and talking. Muldoon figured it would be time before Schmidt would get around to why he wanted to see him.

"Did you see the dumbass Bears Sunday?" He asked Muldoon while taking a drink. "How can you win without a quarterback? They are so cheap, so pathetic. You know I use to have season tickets to those clowns, but I got rid of them. I'll tell you why too. I will accept that teams will have some good years and some bad, but it should balance out. With the dumbass Bears you may have five good years, intermingled with twenty-five bad ones. Bunch of cheap bastards.

"And that World Series," Schmidt didn't miss a beat, "Why don't they just start the games at one in the morning and save everyone the grief?"

Muldoon could only agree. The last time the Bears were really any good was sometime in the 80's. And then baseball seemed to be off in its own little world.

"This place has good burgers," Schmidt said changing the subject. "And the Manhattans aren't bad either." He laughed.

Muldoon took in his surroundings. Place was starting to fill with both Loop shoppers and those working in the area.

"So is there any specific reason you wanted to see me?" Muldoon was getting more curious.

"How's the reverend?"

"Mean Bosco?"

"The one and only. Can you believe that shit Larry? Here is a priest, leaves to get married, and now wants to get divorced. Just how in the hell does that work?" Schmidt shook his head in wonderment.

"He also wants an annulment so he can become a priest again"

107

"Well that should give Rome something to do besides settle law suits."

"Haven't really given it much thought," Muldoon told him. Though Muldoon had a brother for a priest he always tried to lay low when talk turned to religion.

The waitress dropped by took their orders and a second drink order from Schmidt. "You got a brother a priest, don't you?" He asked.

"Yeah."

"Does he fool around?"

"Christ, I don't know never thought about it." Muldoon simply figured he respected his vows and lived his life accordingly. Never any reason to think otherwise.

"Bet he doesn't, probably too decent." Schmidt said swirling the ice in his glass. "The Church is going to Hell in a hand basket. Take my word. Hell when I was a kid, hell even a young man, everything under the sun was a sin. Miss mass on Sunday, doomed to Hell. Ate a stinkin' hot dog on Friday, doomed to Hell. Didn't fast from midnight till you received Communion, doomed to Hell. Touch the Host with your hand, doomed to Hell. Now they have people dealing it out like they are in a canasta tournament.

"Shit anyone can give out Communion. I see guys up there with vasectomies practicing birth control like you wouldn't believe wheeling and dealing with the body and blood. I hope your brother hangs the bastard."

"I don't think my brother has anything to do with it. He is off in Rome teaching young seminarians and the like the joys of celibacy."

"Well that shouldn't take long as there is very little joy in that."

Muldoon looked for the waitress hoping she would show up quickly with the food so he could eat and be gone. Muldoon usually spent his lunch break in his cubicle, alone, doing nothing. If the day was nice he would take a walk, but rarely talked religion during lunch. He liked the lunch break as it gave him time to get away from the phones and the other daily bullshit of an office.

She arrived carrying a platter of food and Schmidt's drink. Their booth becomes quiet as both go about the task of garnishing their burgers.

Muldoon takes a bite just as Schmidt asks, "You are probably wondering why I asked you here?"

Muldoon could only nod.

"I hear they offered you Omaha."

Another nod.

"I think that Marlin Perkins was out there."

Here we go again Muldoon thought while swallowing.

"I saw that son of a bitch wrestle an Anaconda once. Most exciting TV in the history of the medium. Damn thing must have been 40 feet long and it was all wrapped around old Marlin like a big ribbon. The poor bastard is wrestling this damn snake while his buddy Jim, or whoever, is off somewhere describing the action."

"Marlin has his hands full here, but if he can simply get the snake up on shore.... Whoops..... Marlin just went under."

"The whole damn thing scared the living shit out of me. The shit you remember, eh?" He takes a bite and wipes his mouth.

"Anyway Omaha is a nice city. Never been there but I am sure it is nice but I was wondering have you ever thought you might like to be on the other side. You know the agency side?"

Muldoon has thought about this a few times. Nothing serious though. Those on the company side always said that the agency side is where the real money is. He never felt he could live on a commission basis though. As much as he complained about CMI it did offer some security even though that could end any minute as they seemed more concerned about getting rid of people rather than selling and writing insurance.

"Thought about it a couple of times, but that is about all." Muldoon told him.

"How would you like to join up with me?"

"And be your son?" Muldoon smiled.

"No no," he waves a hand at Muldoon. "I am getting up there. Hell I will be sixty three before long and my daughters have no interest in the business, and the guys they married all nice fellows but they are all in that technology shit. They helped with my computers, and I do have a good computer system, but they have no experience in dealing with people. Hell I doubt if they could carry on a conversation. I know I can barely talk to them and I make my living talking. They make their living looking at blank computer screens and wondering why? They are basically illiterate when it comes to dealing with other people. Sad but true." He makes a frown as if to emphasis the point then takes another bite.

This somewhat catches Muldoon by surprise. Schmidt had a nice agency had a nice mix of business between personal and commercial lines. He was out in the Schaumburg area right about the time it started to take off so he was in the right place at the right time. At one time he had three other producers in the agency with him, but one died. Now one is part time and there is Fred.

"What about Fred?"

"Oh Fred is a good guy but he couldn't run an agency. He has all he can do to tie his shoes and make it to the office, but he can sell damn near anything. God the guy is amazing when it comes to selling shit. Plus he too is getting up there. He is only fifty-five but I know he isn't going to stay around forever. Shit he has the first penny he ever made plus he has a place out in Arizona so he can watch the lame Cubbies, as he calls those inept bastards, in Spring Training."

"Why don't you sell it?" Muldoon was thinking that Schmidt could get a good six figures for the agency. "You could stay on as a consultant and get paid for doing nothing."

"I do nothing now but if I can find a young guy like you, how old are you anyway?"

"Thirty seven."

"Perfect age. Well if I can find a young guy like you to come on, give you a nice salary and a piece of the action could help you make it grow. Never replaced Bill when he died. Never really had too. A lot of automation, computers do a lot, that is where my anti social son in laws help out but there is a lot of business out there to be had. I figure new blood could help get it."

Muldoon pushed his plate away and finished off his lemonade. He was thinking about it but he wasn't sure. "What if you kick off, who gets what then. Your wife will want something, and though your daughters may not be interested in the business part of it now I am sure they will like the money part of it."

"They know what I'm doing. You would buy in, within 5 years if we set it up right you could have controlling interest. Plus I have given them a shit load of money and me and the old lady are set. With all these lawyers running about you can do almost anything legally to make everyone happy."

Muldoon was thinking about it, as it was an intriguing offer. But if one of Schmidt's daughters balked, or one of the goofs they married did there might be a lot of headache especially if old Harold here checked out before his time.

"I don't know, how much you offering?" Might as well see what is up Muldoon thought to himself.

"Start you at a base of $40,000 a year. Let you have dead Bill's book of business which would give you about another $85,000. Plus whatever you sold on your own We would set up a pay back scheme where I would give you a certain percentage to come on board and then you would buy the rest on a monthly basis."

One hundred and twenty five fuckin' thousand dollars was all Muldoon could think. The money must be on the agency side. He would never make that at CMI unless he really sucked up and lied and backstabbed everyone he had worked with.

Schmidt continued, "And these idiotic insurance companies have contingencies we would earn which would jack up you income not to mention some of the contests they offer. Hell Fred went to Hawaii one year because of GC's generosity. He sold a shit load of High Valued Homeowners. A lot of those goddam big homes out here now course none worth a shit now but so what. Many start at over half a million. Anyway think about it Larry could offer some real potential for you."

The waitress came by picked up their plates and Schmidt told her he needed one more drink and Muldoon decided to have a beer. He needed a drink.

"Why me?"

"Cause I like you. You have always been fair with me when we have had dealings. You don't hem and haw. You seem to want to get things done. Not like Roundtree who is very thorough but never closes anything out. He always has to check *one more thing.* It is always 'let me check on it and I will get back to you'. Then the damn *one more thing* leads to another *one more thing.* Shit, it never ends. It is like the word closure is not in his vocabulary"

* * *

Nancy knew all the short cuts. She was on Route 53 then she was off on some side street, then back on 53 then on Golf Road over to the Woodfield Mall. The restaurant was behind the Mall where a group of chain restaurants were located. She found a spot next to a handicapped spot near the door.

"Smoking or non smoking?"

"Whatever you have." Neither Sarah nor Nancy were paranoid about smokers. They didn't smoke and didn't believe in all the second hand smoke gibberish. When they went out to eat, they wanted to sit and eat, not sit and wait. Anyway smokers now were so embarrassed that they smoked they were not a bother at all.

They were given a booth next to a window and no sooner were they seated than a male emerged, "hi my name is Bruno and I will be your server. Can I get you ladies something to drink?"

"Bruno? That really your name?" Nancy looked at him with arched brows

Bruno was one big muscle that spoke. A big muscle that fit the description tall, dark and handsome. "It certainly is sweetie and what is yours if I may be so bold."

"You may. My name is Nancy," she smiled, "and this is my friend Sarah."

Bruno the Muscle gave them a wink and a smile. "Your drink order please."

"I will have a raspberry iced tea."

"Same here."

"Excellent choice," Bruno told them with a big smile. "It is my favorite as well." He then was gone.

Nancy let out a sigh. "I don't think he is queer, but then again he might be. He had keys on a loop attached to his belt buckle."

"You think everyone is queer."

"Well today everyone damn near is. But Bruno does have one nice body. It would be a waste if he only ran on DC."

Sarah smiled. She did not care who was straight and who wasn't. All she wanted today was to talk to Nancy about moving. "Larry and I may be moving to Omaha?"

"Really? What's in Omaha?"

"Larry was offered a promotion that would take him to Omaha and we are now debating on whether we should go or not."

"Well or course you should go. Why would you stay?"

Nancy could make everything so simple. Just hearing her saying it made it sound simple. "Well we want to sure we do the right thing."

Bruno returned with the iced tea and the smile. "Nancy and Sarah ready to order yet?" He asked.

"We need a little more time Bruno. Give us five." Nancy said giving him a sweet smile. She was smittened.

He smiled and sauntered off.

"Never been to Omaha," Nancy said. "That insurance company had that TV show called *Wild Kingdom* or some such that I remember watching with my parents. They were always wrestling something on that show. They could never simply capture any animal they always had to wrestle it. Kind of strange now that I think about it."

"That is what my dad said. He use to watch it too."

Nancy picked up a menu. "So what is the hang-up? It is not that far. Not like you would be moving off the end of the earth. I think it is even the same time zone. I have a theory that if you don't change time zones you haven't moved.

"This Central Time zone is great. Detroit was eastern standard and that sucks. Worst time zone in the world. Everything happens at midnight or later. I like being here just because of the time zone. Everything comes on TV at a reasonable hour."

Sarah never thought about time zones. Then she wondered if she should add this to her list, and is it a plus or a minus. "Well I'm worried about my parents."

"Fuck-em. That is what Bob and I decided to do when we moved. If you worry about what everyone thinks you will never do anything with your life. You do what you think is best for you and if someone don't like it, well fuck-em."

She certainly knew how to make things simple Sarah thought. Sarah didn't have that gift. She worried about what people thought especially her parents. "I'm concerned about my parents."

"Fuck-em. They'll get over it. Anyway when Bob and I moved we thought our parents would take it hard. Hell, now they are always making plans to come and see us. I think we see them more now than when we lived in Detroit. If I knew I was going to see them this much I may have stayed in Detroit." She laughed.

"You ladies decide?" Bruno the Muscle had very white teeth. Probably used those strips.

They both decided on a Chef's salad.

"Excellent choice." He sauntered off.

"All men should be that easy to please." Nancy said.

Sarah looked around the restaurant and spotted a couple almost kiddy corner from her but behind Nancy. It was an older man with a younger woman. He looked quite pleased with his acquisition and she seemed to be pleased with being acquired. He was wearing a wedding right, and she wasn't. She supposed they could work together but there was way too much touching, winking and smiling for that.

"Drop a fork and take a look behind you to your right. Old guy young girl."

Nancy did as instructed. She spots them instantly a girl about 25, blonde, slender and perky, they are always perky. The man 50-55, a lot of hair that has been colored, gold jewelry, they always have some type of gold jewelry and what appears to be more teeth than your average human being. All sterling white.

"If he can't score with that or vice versa they are two losers. I wonder where his wife his."

"Maybe with some guy?"

"She is probably home washing his dirty underwear and wondering if the slob is going to take her out to dinner tonight or should she take something out of the freezer."

Bruno arrives with their orders.

"Do you know the two love birds?" Nancy asks while tossing her head in their direction and giving Bruno a smile.

Bruno winks and leans over and whispers to them, "Sidney, the Jewish Wonder, and Yvette his Gentile poon tang. Between you ladies and me it is felt that Yvette will have his money before he has her poon tang."

"You think so," Sarah whispers back. "He looks like he has plans to get lucky."

"Not all plans lead to fulfillment," he tells them. "Take my word for it." He then departs with another knowing wink and smile.

"Our boy Bruno must know something that we don't" Nancy says.

Sarah nods in agreement

* * *

Cyrus Gladkowski owned a body shop in Gurnee, one in Lombard and one on the southeast side of Chicago. He spent his time equally between all three or at least tried to though going to the southeast side of Chicago was not a priority. His father started the business in Chicago and once Cy, as he liked to be called, took over the business after his father's death Cy expanded. First the shop in Lombard 17 years ago and then Gurnee 10 years ago. He basically kept the Chicago location for sentimental reasons, as his mother did not want to give up the original location. How a body shop could have sentimental value was beyond Cy, but she let him run the business as he saw fit so why rock the boat? She was now 78 years old and would not be around much longer. When she died so would the Chicago location. He had a buyer for it, Emanuel Jackson a shine he hired 15 years ago and for the most part honest or at least as honest as Cy and who had made inquiries about buying it. The agreement was that once Mrs. Gladkowski checked out Emanuel could check in.

John Bosco tracked down Gladkowski in Lombard. Gladkowski was sitting behind his desk in his office off of the customer waiting room. There were no customers here. The only time a customer would be here was when they were dropping off a car or picking one up or waiting for an inflated estimate. The chairs in the waiting room were metal kitchen chairs that appeared to be at least 45 years old. The vinyl was worn and the metal was rusted. Some out of date magazines scattered on two old end tables one holding a lamp with a lopsided window shade.

The furniture in the office was mix of metal, wood and plastic. His desk was gray metal, his chair was wood and there were a couple of old plastic chairs that Gladkowski use to have on his patio. There was to the left a window that looked out to the parking lot. Why Gladkowski was successful no one could really figure out, but his body shop looked like what most people thought a body shop should look like.

Gladkowski was getting ready to light a cigar when Bosco walked in. Gladkowski was built like a fireplug, square and solid. The match was at the end of the cigar when he noted Bosco. Bosco and Gladkowski had done a lot of work together. Bosco would recommend one of Gladkowski's places for a bit of the action or as some would say a kick back.

"John Bosco, what brings you to our fair city?" He said looking up.

"I got to talk to you." Bosco seemed a bit nervous and passed a hand over his balding head.

A plume of smoke was now around Gladkowski's head, "what about?"

Bosco pulled up a green plastic chair and sat across from Gladkowski, "well, as you know I am in the process of getting divorced and then if all goes according to plan the marriage will be annulled and I will then become a priest again."

"Miracles never cease." Gladkowski thought he had heard it all, but this was the topper. He was convinced that Bosco was nuts but a nut that would harm no one, simply nuts. A lot of religious people or those who thought they were religious were nuts. You could pick up any newspaper and have that verified. Organized religion may well be the worst thing that happened to man. Gladkowski was convinced it was the root of all evil in the world. Gladkowski believed in god, but he did not get carried away. He too, like Bosco was a Catholic. He was what the so-called good Catholics called a lapsed Catholic. He didn't care. He had convinced himself it was all pretty much bullshit. Now what he had just heard pretty much clinched it.

He had grown up on the south side of Chicago in the Gage Park area a Polish neighborhood where religion was an important part of the community. He had been through Catholic grammar and high schools, basically the whole nine yards. But at some point in his early adult life he came to the conclusion that enough is enough. You should be able to believe and pray to god without a rule for every occasion. Gladkowski was pretty much convinced if Christ returned to earth the first thing he would do would be to eliminate 99.9999% of the rules.

"So I need some help." Bosco said matter of factly slowly building his confidence.

"In what way?" Gladkowski said while letting another plume of smoke drift from his mouth and wondering what the nut was thinking.

"Money."

"You want a loan?"

"No, then I would have to pay you back. I was thinking we could come to another arrangement." Last thing Bosco wanted was to owe Gladkowski money that he would have to pay back. He didn't want to have to pay anyone back. His plan was very simple, get divorced, get it annulled, and get back in the Church's good graces. Very cut and dried.

"And that would be what?" Gladkowski leaned back in his chair as if to get comfortable listening to whatever Bosco was about to hatch.

"Well," Bosco said looking around.

"There is no one around John, relax." Gladkowski told him. What a nut.

"I need a bigger kickback."

"For Christ sake I give you a hundred bucks a car now that you bring to us."

"I'm going to need more."

"How much more?"

"At least one seventy five a car."

"Jesus Christ."

"Please don't swear."

Gladkowski stood up behind his desk. Bosco was nuts no doubt about it. It was easy to pad an estimate a couple of hundred bucks or so but you couldn't get too goofy or things would get noticed. Even the shine Emanuel Jackson knew that. Never get greedy.

"Jesus Christ Bosco we have a nice little thing going here. Don't get greedy."

"It won't be for long. I just need it for my divorce and annulment."

Gladkowski sat back down and took a long drag on his cigar. God was he nuts. *A divorce and an annulment.* Where is god when you need him? "How much more?"

"I figure one seventy five a car." Bosco repeated.

"For you?"

"Yeah."

"For how long?"

"Forty cars."

"Jesus H. Christ you know how many cars that is?"

"Please don't swear, and I do know how much forty is." Bosco was becoming assertive, as he wanted the money. "I figure with three shops we can do it in three months, give or take."

Gladkowski went quiet thinking about it. The guy was definitely nuts. "Let me ask you something. You want to become a priest again, is that right?"

"God willing."

"Well I am sure he can't wait." Gladkowski said. No doubt about it Bosco definitely needed a roof job. "But to do this you are willing to steal. The last time I checked John, and I am not a religious man, but I do believe stealing is a sin."

"But it can be forgiven."

"Really?"

"A confession here a penance there and I'm back in the saddle again so to speak."

"Praise the Lord."

"I hope to."

Gladkowski didn't mind skimming. Every time he gave Bosco a hundred he took hundred. To get one seventy five he would have to raise the estimates by three to four hundred bucks a car, even more. Couldn't do this on cars with simple damage, but it could be done and maybe even in the time frame Bosco wanted. If customers balked he could blame inflation or increased insurance costs. As matter of fact Gladkowski loved telling that to adjusters from various insurance companies, "If you bastards keep raising my rates I'm going to be out of business." He would tell them. They would ignore him and change the subject.

"So how much does a divorce and annulment and reinstatement in the priesthood cost a sinner like you?"

"I don't know yet but I may have a connection in Rome."

"No shit Rome? Right to the top. The Pope?"

"A brother of a friend." Bosco didn't want to tell Gladkowski it was a co-worker for fear he would put two and two together and get Muldoon involved. Too many cooks could spoil the broth and all that shit.

Gladkowski did some quick math in his head. "Forty cars will come to $7,000 for you. Is that the going rate to buy into heaven?" Gladkowski laughed. He also figured if he did it right it would come to $7,000 for him as well. But he doubted if it would buy him a ticket to heaven.

"I'll have to think about it John," he told him. "After all I'm not always here when the cars come in, but I suppose we can work something out. When do you need to know?"

"The sooner the better. I just can't wait to preach again."

"Jesus Christ."

"Please don't swear."

"Actually it is easier than stealing."

***

Muldoon was sitting in his cubicle thinking about his lunch with Schmidt when Robinson walked in.

"You hear the news?"

"What news?"

"More cutbacks."

"Who is going to do the work?" Muldoon figured they simply couldn't continue to let people go. If they did no one would be left. There were always rumors about more people being let go, but no one dwelled on them as everyone hoped that was all they were rumors.

"The white power structure does not care. Their only concern is lining their pockets." Trevayne stated with a certain satisfaction.

"Blacks don't line their pockets?" Muldoon wondered.

'We gots no pockets to line," Robinson lets out a laugh. There were times when he even knew when he was full of shit.

"If they offer me a severance deal I'm taking it," he said. "I am really tired of the bullshit. Anyway I want my social security before they give it all to the Cubans."

"What Cubans?" Muldoon looked around. "There are no Cubans here."

"The ones in Florida for crissake. You know they come over here not knowing shit from Shinola. No job, don't speak the language, never contributed a penny to the system, don't know their asses from holes in the ground, yet they get social security benefits. Then these asshole politicians wonder why it is going broke. Jesus, how dumb can they be."

This sounded so stupid it had to be true, but Muldoon did not care to talk about Cubans just now. "Where did you hear about the layoffs?"

"The luscious Vicki. I don't know what the hell she does here, but she always knows what is going on. Not only a good looking white woman but a smart one as well. Five percent are going to be canned. She had it right the last time and I am sure she has right this time."

All Muldoon could think was, where will it all end? No wonder things don't get done during normal business hours people are too worried to work.

Then Trevayne sat down looking exhausted. "You know something Larry, I am glad I'm old. No offense but I would hate to be your age. Your generation is screwed. By the time your retirement gets here, there will be no money. All the deadbeats will have it. And the dumb politicians that gave it to them will all be wringing their hands, as if they care, the phony bastards.

"When I started here I knew I could make it to the end. Being black helped but I looked around. There were people here with thirty plus years of service when I started. Now, I'm it. Once I'm gone the longest tenured employee could be you."

Muldoon never thought about that but Robinson was probably right.

"Roundtree has been with about 4 companies in the past 15 years even Doris has been around the block once or twice. I'm only here because I be black. There have been many a time over the past

30 years I wished I was white so I could move on. It ain't easy being black and competent. You can never get fired. Hell it isn't even easy to be black and incompetent. You can never get fired." Robinson let out a sigh, "you know that dope Jesse Jackson and the idiot Sharpton they do more harm than good."

"I thought that was a given."

"It is but don't tell no one where you heard it."

SIX

Bosco was sitting on his recliner trying to decide if he should turn on David Letterman or Jay Leno. However he did not have his remote which was out of reach on the coffee table and he didn't feel like getting up to get it. He also wanted a beer but that would mean he would have to get out of the chair for that as well. He decided to stay put. He wanted to think and TV and a beer would simply interrupt his thought processes.

His divorce was moving along slowly but moving. His future ex was not putting up too much of a fight. They didn't have much to fight for, no kids, very little savings and some furniture. Bosco didn't care if she got everything as long as she was out of his life. Sheila had a new squeeze so she would probably be glad to be rid of him

The annulment part could be tricky though. She might balk at that. She was good in bed but had a temper. If she wanted to make trouble she would. He had yet to tell her that once the divorce came down he was going for an annulment to get back in god's good graces. She would have to be a part of that. He knew she would laugh at him and call him one stupid jackass, but he had to do what he knew was right. He decided he would cross that bridge when he came to it.

He hadn't spoken to her in quite a while, almost six months. They spoke thru their attorneys. They were now supposed to be in some type of cooling off period as if someone actually believed two people who could no longer stand each other were going to get back together. Where do people come up with this idiocy?

There was a time when they were in love not only love but lust. It had all started so innocently. She walked thru the gym stopped to watch him, gave him a smile and said hi. He said hi back and smiled shyly. He was nervous around women; he never had a real date. He kissed a girl once or twice, but once he entered the seminary his dating days were over.

To this day he doesn't know what possessed him but before he knew it he asked her if she would like to go out for some coffee. Then the coffee led to a drink. The drink to dinner, dinner to her apartment, her apartment to her bed, her bed to guilt, guilt to shame, shame to love, love to a promise of happily every after, happily ever after to 6 months of bliss and then a slow descent into hell on earth.

There was an attraction there but he didn't want to rehash it anymore. There were many times he thought of calling her, to feel her out but he felt if he stayed out of sight and sound he would eventually be out of her thoughts completely and then the annulment would be easier to accomplish. Why should she care anyway? She has what she wants.

He would have to get a hold of Muldoon's brother in Rome. That would be a good connection to have. Bosco knew the church could be bought. How do all those mob guys get buried in Catholic Cemeteries? The world think they all had death bed confessions? *A dollar here a dollar there and we can plant you anywhere,* was pretty much how it worked.

He would have to suck up to Muldoon. Get his brothers email in Rome. That would be a nice cheap way to get a hold of him.

Type a little note.

Plant the seed.

Ask him, if by chance he would be coming to the states for a visit and maybe get together. But now Muldoon might be going to Omaha. He remembered some TV show that Mutual of Omaha out there had. Had to do with animals. He knew absolutely nothing about Omaha. He would have to work on Muldoon before he left.

Maybe when he got back in god's good graces he could go to Rome, the Eternal City. See where St. Peter was buried. Start hanging around with the in crowd of the Church. He would have to brush up on his Italian. He knew some not much. The Church frowned on America's hierarchy, not their money, just their ways. Perhaps he could change all that. Maybe with his influence there would indeed some day be an American Pope. Right now the Church was not ecumenical enough for an American Pope. They were all talk but no action. He could change that.

He knew he couldn't talk to the local Bishop as he was all wrapped up in that pedophilia shit. Bosco's scheme would probably make the Bishop's head spin. Make the Bishop wish he was a Presbyterian. But then again he might be relieved he doesn't have to deal with another sex scandal. The last time he talked to the Bishop it was about leaving the priesthood to get married. He thought the poor guy was going to have a stroke. Called him an asshole and told Bosco he would probably rot in hell. At the time love and sex seemed better than hell so Bosco ignored the advice.

At least he hadn't got involved in pedophilia. Thank god he never had the urge that way. That was sick. Fortunately that never crossed his mind. Adultery had crossed his mind, and he acted on it and he had to admit he and Sheila were good at it. He remembered one time someone asking Sheila if they practiced birth control and she said, "No, we have it down pat". The more Bosco thought about it that may have been the last time she made him laugh. Then she met Arnold. Arnold was athletic, had a lot of hair, a lot of white even teeth and could fix things. Where Bosco was losing hair, couldn't fix anything, and simply had ordinary teeth.

Now he was simply an ex priest who felt guilt every day, losing his hair, and couldn't fix much of anything, living alone in this small one bedroom apartment. No social life to speak of. His parents were deceased, and his sister lived in California and they spoke only at the Holidays. She wouldn't care what he did anyway.

The priests he knew when he was a priest are either lonesome or moved on or being arraigned.

He had lost touch with just about everyone with the exception of his co-workers at CMI. Muldoon seemed to be the only that was civil to him. Tucker and the luscious Vicki Higgins would call him Reverend or Father. Like those two had a pipeline to God.

He also knew that Gladkowski thought he was nuts. But you only get one chance at life, and you got to get it right. He knew, beyond all doubt, that he should be a priest. He made his mistake, and now wanted to fix it. He just had to get back in, and if all went according to plan he would.

* * *

They had waited for the kids to fall asleep before they made love. When they were finished they cuddled for a moment, talked quietly and simply fell asleep. Now at 5AM Muldoon was awake.

Sarah was sound asleep, as were the kids. Muldoon lay there looking at the ceiling and thinking of Omaha and the pending cut backs.

He spoke with Vicki before leaving the office and she was told by a source in the Home Office that there would be more cut backs. No one questioned Vicki's sources. Everyone figured with her looks and her personality it was probably some guy who simply liked talking to her and trying to get on her good side.

According to Vicki the layoffs were going to be on the West Coast. Mainly California and Washington state with a few scatterings her and there. It was the here and there that made Muldoon think. Sounded like some Branch Managers were going to be given the boot. Muldoon had nothing to base this on it was only a hunch.

If CMI was going to cut people on what seemed like an almost monthly basis maybe he should simply forget about Omaha and take Schmidt up on his offer or start looking elsewhere. He had told Sarah about the cut backs, figuring they wouldn't be offering him a promotion if they were going to lay him off. She was more concerned about the move to Omaha and didn't seem concerned about more cut backs.

He thought the adventure of moving could be fun. Omaha wasn't Chicago in size but it could be a nice change. No major league sports and there were those that could argue that Chicago didn't have any either, at least until the White Sox decided to end the drought. Black Hawks finally won something. Bulls are history and the Bears are dead in the water still looking for their ever-elusive quarterback.

He was sure Omaha had golf courses, grocery stores, malls, movie theaters, schools, paved streets and normal people. Pretty much all you needed to survive He knew they had a zoo. Every city has a zoo some kind of rule.

Sarah let out a sigh. He turned to look at her. He was a lucky man. She not only was a good wife and a good mother, simply a good person. He was probably biased but then the truth is the truth.

The phone rang.

Scared the hell out of him. Had to stop and collect himself to figure out what it was.

Rang again.

He jumped out of bed and raced over to the dresser to answer it.

"Hello." He tried to make it sound like he was always up and alert at five AM at the same time wondering who it was.

"You sitting down?" It was his sister Marie in Columbus. She sounded very down.

"What is it?"

"Dad is dead."

His knees buckled. He stopped breathing. His mind racing backward with memories and forward with what happens now? He had to sit.

She continued, "Mom called, he went for a checkup and a hospital killed him. I called Frank in Rome. He will be here as soon as he can. You will have to get a hold of Tom in California."

"A hospital killed him?" How does that happen he wondered.

"I'm leaving this morning to fly down to Mom to help make arrangements to bring the body back here. When I have further information I will call you. You will have to call the Funeral Parlor and make arrangements."

She was so damn organized it was scary. "Slow down," he said.

"Dad died. He went in for a checkup and never came home. Seventy four years old you go for a check up and they kill you."

His thinking was screwed up. A hospital killed him? Why was that all he could think. Finally, "How's Mom?"

"As well as can be expected. She has some friends with her. She sounded kind of numb, but I should be able to get down there by two. I will call tonight."

She was gone. His head was spinning. He hung up the phone and sat on the edge of the bed. He was emotionless.

"What is it?" Sarah asked.

"Was Marie. My dad died."

She was quiet for a moment as if she had to let the news set in, "Oh Larry I am so sorry." She slid over next to him and put an arm around him. She saw the tears starting to form in his eyes. She felt them in her eyes. "What happened?"

"I don't know Marie said the hospital killed him."

She didn't understand it either. She grabbed her robe. "I'll make some coffee." She felt that he wanted to be alone.

He stared at his feet. He had goofy looking toes. What was so important a bit a go now didn't seem important at all. Omaha seemed like a distant memory. Job cut backs didn't even matter. How could he be dead, *a hospital killed him?* Marie always somewhat dramatic.

He didn't move for a quarter of an hour

Sarah let him be. She couldn't believe it. She made the coffee as if a robot. Walked to a drawer and got a pencil and some paper.

You try to do what is right

Every morning, noon and night.

You love each other as you should.

Through all the bad and all the good.

The children come, you buy a home

You can't remember being alone.

You both work hard to make it work

No responsibility do you shirk.

Your kids grow up as they should

And turn out like you knew they would.

But no one tells you about the worst.

That one of you must leave first.

It wasn't much but it much but it made her feel better. She thought of Larry and herself. One of them would die first and leave the other behind. If there was a flaw in the system that was it.

SEVEN

Tucker was at his desk at 7AM. This was unusual for he made it a point not to arrive until after 8. He felt by coming in a bit late each day everyone would simply think he was busy visiting an agent, or checking a piece of property or doing something productive for CMI instead of being at home eating bran.

He was early this morning for the simple reason he couldn't sleep. He was going to lie there, but then his wife Delores started snoring. He poked her a few times but it was like trying to stop a runaway freight. He reluctantly decided to take a shower and come into the office before he went deaf.

He was sitting at his desk looking at some papers that were scattered there and waiting for someone to come in and make the coffee. There were a few people in the office, but the coffee duties were the responsibility of the clerical department and none of them had yet arrived. Seeing that this was Wanda, the dip in charge of clerical, area of expertise no one would interfere as no one wanted the wrath of Wanda to descend upon them. Wanda was very protective of her turf.

He saw Doris Simpson walking towards his office looking like a nun who had forgotten her habit. What a plain looking woman he thought. He briefly wondered why she was in so early, but then he remembered she was a hard worker so she probably came in to do some work. She probably was not too concerned about someone snoring as she lived alone and he wasn't sure if lesbians snored.

She stopped at his doorway, "I have a voice mail from Roundtree. He is going to South America."

"What? Did you say South America?" Tucker wasn't sure if he heard her right.

"He left a voice mail and is going to South America." She made it sound like an everyday occurrence. "He tried to talk his son out of becoming an attorney, but his son told him if not an attorney then a journalist. Roundtree felt that there was no longer a reason to stay here anymore as everything is going to hell in a hand basket. So he went to South America." Doris presented this bit of news in business-like fashion as she did with all happenings in the office.

"Is he quitting?" Tucker was hoping that he wasn't quitting, as then he would have to interview people, read their lying resumes and listen to their phony bullshit. How he hated to interview people. It was a fate worse than death.

"He didn't say, he simply told me to pass it on and he will get to you as soon as he can."

"South America?" Tucker simply shook his head and thought to himself, and I got up early for this.

"That's what he said."

"Because his son is becoming an attorney?"

"Or a journalist."

"Two good reasons, but he should have given some notice." It was the little things that counted. No one cared about the little things.

Now what was going to happen to the workflow? Tucker was going to have to make some managerial decisions now that they were short an underwriter. He hated making managerial decisions as they always turned out wrong. Why couldn't Roundtree just quit and go to South America. There is probably some stupid rule somewhere that says if an employee gets up and heads for South America with no notice, and no return date you must hold his job open till he is declared missing or dead.

"Is clerical here yet," he wanted some coffee.

"A couple of them just arrived. What do you want me to do with   Roundtree's   files?"

He didn't know. He didn't have a clue. It was too early for Tucker to make a decision. "Let me think about it and we'll come up with something."

Doris knew he didn't have a clue. She simply told him okay and walked away.

Tucker went back to staring at the papers on his desk. South America? Why would anyone go to South America? Sounds like something Roundtree would do. Goddam Indian. He gathered the papers on his desk and put them in a neat little pile. He felt as if just accomplished something.

"You got a minute?"

Tucker looked up and it was Trevayne Robinson. All Tucker could think was didn't anyone sleep in anymore? Did everyone come in early? "Yeah."

"I came to give my notice."

Tucker simply stared at him. "Your notice?"

"I be retiring."

Now I am going to have to interview a jig was all Tucker could think. They all think the world owes them a living because allegedly everyone in their family at one time or another was a slave. Then they talk that street gibberish and have that goofy hair. "What brought this on?" First Roundtree and now Robinson.

Robinson entered the office and sat across from Tucker. "The luscious Vicki Higgins says there are more cut backs coming.

If they don't offer me an out I am leaving at the end of the year. The wife and I have had enough."

"More cut backs?" Tucker sounded surprised

"That is what Vicki says." It did not surprise Robinson that Tucker knew nothing about the layoffs as generally speaking Tucker knew nothing.

"When is the end of the year?"

"A little over two months, or December 31st to be exact."

"Is clerical here yet?" He needed some coffee.

"They started to make coffee right before I came to see you." Robinson too was waiting for the coffee to be brewed.

"I need some coffee." With that Tucker walked out of his office and down to the break room. On his way he passed Vicki's cubicle but it was empty. He had no idea when she started, as she seemed to have her own hours. He spotted Bernie walking to his cubicle. "We are going to be short of help for a while."

Bernie simply looked at Tucker, made no response. Seemed to accept the fact that they would be short of help and seemed not to care. He continued to his cubicle. Why couldn't that goof go to South America Tucker wondered.

Tucker continued to the break room and got his coffee and returned to his office. Vicki was still not in and Robinson was still in his office. "You need something?" Tucker asked him.

"No, just wanted to give you my notice."

"Put something in writing."

"Will there be an exit interview?"

Tucker took a sip from his coffee. Exit interviews were even dumber than job interviews. The only good thing about them was you didn't have to read someone's stupid resume just had listen to them gripe.

"I suppose."

"Well I gots some things I gots to tell them."

Smokes were simply a pain in the ass, and then they wonder why they don't get ahead. Like this goof actually thinks someone in the Home Office gives a flying fuck on what he has to say. No one on the planet cares what he has to say so why would Home Office? They don't care what anyone has to say, but I am the one who has to listen to it Tucker thought. All the quitters tell you the same thing. They would have stayed but they just weren't treated with respect and they were given too much responsibility for too little pay. Just the thought of it made Tucker almost want to weep. "I am sure you have all kinds of words of wisdom for them Trevayne"

"Thats I do." With that he got up but before leaving he said, "Should I email it to you or just place it on your desk?"

"What?"

"My resignation."

"Both." Tucker didn't know why he would need both but there was probably a rule somewhere that you should have two.

"No problem." Robinson sounded as if the weight of the world was now off his shoulders

Tucker watched him walk away and thought to himself maybe Trevayne was the lucky ones. Getting out with his sanity or what was left of it. Wanting an exit interview made Tucker wonder if Robinson was sane. Why should someone that is leaving give a damn about that? No one paid attention to them. Just some Human Resource bullshit. But then again if a Black doesn't have something to whine about they whine. A very vicious circle they are in.

Tucker was going to log onto his computer, mainly to read the paper, but he knew that if he did he would be tempted to look at his email. And some of it would require a reply something he was not up to doing. His phone rang.

Who would be calling me now he wondered? He checked his watch just going on 8 a time when he is usually not here. "Joe Tucker, may I help you?"

Muldoon was surprised Tucker picked up. He thought by calling before 8 he would get Tucker's voice mail and simply be able to leave a message without having to talk to him. "Larry Muldoon," he didn't know why he gave his full name but he felt if he simply said Larry, Tucker wouldn't know who it was. And he felt that he should say more than Muldoon. "I called to let you know that my father died early this morning and I won't be in for a few days."

Tucker didn't say a thing for about five to six seconds. Two underwriters short was all he could think of. Finally, "sorry Larry he wasn't sick was he?"

"No went in for a checkup and died." Muldoon figured it best to keep things simple as talking to Tucker things could wander.

"A hospital killed him? This is not the first time Larry. They get away with murder. You have my deepest sympathy. If I were you I'd sue the bastards. Take whatever time you need. Do you know the arrangements yet?" Tucker thought that perhaps they should send flowers. Vicki usually took care of those things and she wasn't in yet.

Muldoon was surprised Tucker came to the same conclusion as his sister, or maybe his sister came to the same conclusion as Tucker. Muldoon thought best to ignore it. "No. The body should be back here tonight, or no later than tomorrow, and I will make arrangements with the Funeral Home today."

"Well keep us informed, and I would check on that hospital if I were you." There was nothing else to say except good-byes.

Tucker was going to go and look for Vicki to get some flowers for Muldoon and his family. Most of the office staff appeared to be present. He decided instead to take a walk over to Bosco's office and let him know about Muldoon.

"Good morning Joe," Bosco said before Tucker was even in his office.

Cheery bastard must have been that religious upbringing. "Good morning Father. Listen I stopped by to let you know Muldoon's father passed and Larry won't be in for a couple of days. If and when the luscious Vicki shows up, get her to order some flowers. I should have the name of the funeral home later."

"Muldoon's dad died?' Bosco almost sounded joyous.

Tucker noticed. "Don't let it hit you too hard."

"Oh I am saddened." Bosco's mind was racing. Muldoon's dad had died. Praise the Lord. That would mean Muldoon's brother, the priest from Rome, would be here. He could talk to him directly. Make his case, and be in the Church's good graces by the end of the week. . God was indeed watching out for him. Praise the Lord some more.

"Did he say anything about his brother?" Bosco asked.

"Only one dead Muldoon as far as I know," Tucker said.

"His brother is a priest."

"Isn't everyone?"

"No, you don't understand." Bosco didn't know why he was trying to explain himself to Tucker. "Will his brother be here for the funeral?"

"I would think the children would be there. That is how things pretty much work. A dad dies, the kids show up sometimes even a neighbor or two. Next thing you know an in law, then some friends. Pretty soon they are turning people away at the door. That is, unless he was a prick."

"A prick? You hear he was a prick?" Now Bosco was concerned. If Muldoon's dad was a prick then the brother from Rome might not be there.

"Never heard he was a prick. Now my old man was a prick if you want to talk about pricks." Tucker could go on for hours about his old man. He drank too much, cheated on his mother. Eventually left and then came back and repeated the process. Then left and was never seen again.

"You sure?"

"About my old man, damn straight I am."

"No about Muldoon's old man not being a prick."

"I don't know never met the man."

"Then he could have been?"

"Anything is possible." Tucker turned to leave. "Have Vicki order some flowers, something nice and have her stop by to get the address from me." Tucker didn't really care about flowers for Muldoon's old man. Just thought a little extra might get Muldoon over the edge to go to Omaha and help get a feather in his bonnet.

Tucker returned to his office and saw that he had a voice mail. No wonder he never came in early too much shit happened. People leaving, quitting and dying, and now a voice mail. He picked up the phone receiver to hear the message and hoped against hope it didn't mean he was going to have to return a phone call. The message was from David Schwartz, at Home Office, a VP. He was going to be in day after tomorrow to meet with him and Muldoon about Omaha. He also wanted to see Bernie, Doris, Roundtree and Phillips and the rest of the underwriting staff. Some things he wanted to go over.

All Tucker could think was oh shit. Roundtree was on his way or in South America for no apparent reason. Muldoon would be out of the office till his old man was planted. Robinson wanted to pick a fight and that only left, Doris, Bernie and Phillips for the meeting. When Home Office said there were things they wanted *to go over* it only meant bad news. Could be the cut backs, nah he would have heard something by now wouldn't he?

He wondered if he should call Schwartz back and explain Muldoon's situation, but then there was no way to explain Roundtree's situation. He would have to see Vicki. She knew how those asses in suits thought. She might have some advice. Only trouble was he didn't know when she started. The Reverend Bosco might. He told his secretary to get Bosco and have him stop by.

He then logged on his computer. There was a message from Roundtree. He opened and read it

Fuck you Joe.

Well at least he kept it brief.

****

Bosco was like a kid on Christmas. His ship was coming in and he was going to get on it. Muldoon's old man was dead and it was now time to hoist the mainsail. Death is sad, but it must happen to all. And Bosco knew that Muldoon's brother would be here for the funeral. It was all too good to be true. Praying like a crazed man for the past six months was starting to pay off. Sheila would be history. Once he had the marriage annulled it would be like she never existed, just a figment of his imagination. Hell, it might even help save her over sexed and wretched soul.

He simply had to come with some type of plan to get to Muldoon's brother. He would have to be humble but earnest, whatever that meant. He would have to lay it on but not too thick. Let him know that if Rome could intervene and get his marriage annulled and back in the priesthood the world would be a much better place to live. He could go back to giving those pointless sermons each and every Sunday. The ones Catholics have heard over and over and over since the age of six but fear that if they miss one they will burn in Hell forever.

But now he would be able to help married couples. Hell he had been there and done that. He could be the voice of experience. True he and Sheila never had kids, thank god, but he knew the joys of sex as well as the hell of marriage. He would be able to relate. Maybe even give advice to those about to get married. Though what advice he would give he didn't know as once he said, "I do" it was then pretty much downhill.

He said a Hail Mary, as a form of thanks, and went out to look for Vicki. She was in her cubicle paging through a *Cosmopolitan.* "Did you hear about Muldoon's dad?" He asked her while standing in her doorway. She was one good-looking woman. If he hadn't gotten religion she would indeed be a temptation. Her cubicle smelled of some type of perfume that radiated warmth and sexuality. He liked breathing her air.

She looked up, "No what."

He told her and a look of sadness came over her. "Tucker would like you to order some flowers to have them sent to the Funeral Parlor. Get something really nice. Go all out." If we can't impress Muldoon perhaps we can his brother Bosco thought. "Expense should be of no concern. Perhaps of wreath of some type. We should have the address later this afternoon."

She simply nodded and wanted to know what happened. Bosco told her what he knew.

"You mean a hospital killed him?" She sounded somewhat alarmed.

"Well I don't know if they did or not, but that is where he was when he bought the farm."

"Why can't you just say passed away or died. You men at times are so insincere."

Good looking and sweet smelling but still had the unique feminine quality to be a pain in the ass. Sermons from her he did not need, "just order some nice flowers and you should probably send an email to everyone letting them know as I doubt if Tucker will do that."

Tucker left knowing Vicki would do what was needed and then go back to her magazine. He wondered if he should call Gladkowski and see how things were going on the damaged auto front. He should probably let Gladkowski know there was a chance the timetable for reinstatement into the Church's good graces could be headed for the fast track. But he decided to wait and see when Muldoon's brother was going to put in an appearance and when the final plans were in place. He felt he should get some of his ducks in a row before he starts finalizing his plan.

***

Muldoon was having a busy morning. Once he was awaken with the phone call he had no hope of returning to bed. Sarah had made some coffee. She told the kids what had happened and they all took it hard. It was decided to let them stay home from school, but they were told to give their father some peace. Muldoon had spoken with them later that morning and due to the fact they attended Catholic schools death was something they were well aware. As any Catholic knows, you cannot really be a saint unless you are dead.

And the old reliable standby, Grandpa was now in a better place

Actually he was on a plane to O'Hare.

Marie had called one more time and had pretty much taken over the operation of planning the funeral of her father. She was on her way to Florida to get their mother and bring her back to Chicago. Her husband Harry and their 4 children would drive in this afternoon and should arrive sometime early this evening. Marie and their mother would stay with Tom and Sarah and Harry and the kids would stay with Harry's family. She had also gotten a hold of Frank and he would be in touch. Marie told Larry he should make arrangements at the local rectory for Frank. She was going to call the rest of the family, cousins, aunts and uncles, and suggested that Larry and Sarah let those who need to know know. She also instructed Muldoon to contact Tom the chore Muldoon was now carrying out.

The sleepy voice of Tom answered the phone in California.

Muldoon broke the news to his brother and Tom wanted to know if the hospital killed him for if they had he knew some good lawyers in California who love to sue anyone, anything, anytime, anyplace, for any reasonable fee.

"I don't think that is necessary Tom," Muldoon told him

"Keep the option open. A buck is a buck."

Tom told Larry that he would get to Chicago as soon as possible hopefully that evening would rent a car and stay in a local motel. Larry lied and said they had room, but Tom was a loner and he knew that his brother was simply being polite.

He had called to make arrangements to meet the Funeral Director when the phone rang.

Muldoon thought it was probably his sister again, with more instructions, but it was Frank. "How's Mom?" he wanted to know.

Muldoon told him that Marie was going down to be with her but he had talked to her briefly and she seemed fine. Running on adrenaline for now, but once she gets with her family it should be easier for her.

"Well if she is smart she will sue that hospital."

Perhaps some things were hereditary Muldoon thought to himself.

"We don't know what they did, if anything." Larry told him

"Hey you go in to a hospital to have a physical you should be able to walk out alive."

"So how are things in Rome?" Muldoon asked changing the subject.

"Things are goofy. With all that is going on back there we Americans are looked on as a bunch of perverts." Muldoon didn't find that surprising as most Americans were perverts even elected a President that was basically one.

Muldoon didn't feel much like listening so he told Frank he had spoken with Father Harris and things were all set for him to stay up at the rectory of Holy Mother of God Church. The parish Muldoon belonged to.

"Why there? You know I can't stand that guy."

"He is the only priest I know and it is the church we go to."

"You still go? I thought you would have bailed by now. You are not saying that to be nice to me are you?"

"Frank, don't make things any more complicated than they are. It will only be for a few days. He can't be that bad." Maybe it was the vow of celibacy that made priests goofy? And how did he know that weekly mass was pretty much a thing of the past?

"Well he was jerk in the seminary."

Muldoon was of the impression that everyone was a jerk so being told by his brother that a priest was a jerk did not surprise Muldoon in the least. He figured priests, nuns, ministers and just about all religious people were jerks of some type. Might be a couple of exceptions but they were not members of the Muldoon family or of the Muldoon circle of acquaintances.

"You could stay with Tom, but then I don't know where he is staying."

"He is a sexed crazed maniac."

"He's single."

"He should practice some self-control. He probably hasn't told anyone where he is staying as he wants to get laid."

Don't we all thought Muldoon? "Let us know when you get in. I have to go up and see the Funeral Director and make some arrangements. People will be looking forward to seeing the priest from Rome."

Frank let out a groan. Because he was assigned to Rome everyone thought he was buddy buddy with the Pope. Hell, he rarely if ever saw the Pope. He saw some Cardinals here and there, but they were basically grumpy old men who frowned on anything and anyone American. Unless of course they needed something American like a computer or a cell phone or their favorite, cash.

They finished up their conversation and Frank hoped to be in by morning. Muldoon hadn't seen his brother Frank in about 4 years and for whatever reason didn't really miss him. Then he thought he wasn't that close to Marie either. Marie was the oldest and probably the smartest but married herself a real goof in Harry. Harry was a professor of something at Ohio State. Muldoon didn't have much to do with Harry as he still used pocket protectors. Muldoon found that very disconcerting.

It would be good to see Tom. He was a Triple A umpire and doing well. He felt with some luck and hard work he could get to the Majors within a year or two. Tom lived and died baseball. Couldn't play it worth a damn but the loved the game. And he was a bit less serious than Marie and Frank.

Muldoon made a few more calls to some old neighbors to break the news, and all were quite generous in their praise for his dad. Muldoon came to the conclusion that when you reach a certain age you simply learn to be gracious and don't spend too much time looking for a scapegoat. Like no one he called blamed the hospital. They instead blamed god. *Well Larry, when He wants you He takes you.*

* * *

Tucker found Vicki in her cubicle playing Solitaire on her computer. At least she wasn't looking at a porn sight. Tucker was tempted to ask her what she exactly did for CMI but thought better of it. She did work in claims, always on time, rarely missed a day of work, easy on the eyes and always got a good review.

"Did you order the flowers?" He asked.

She turned from her screen to look at him, "They have been ordered and once I have the address I will forward it to the florist." She gave him a smile and his heart skipped a beat and he loved the sweet smell that came from her cubicle.

He was going to ask what she had decided on but knew she would do the right thing. Tucker was more interested in the coming layoffs that Robinson had mentioned. "What did you hear about the new round of layoffs?"

Vicki knew Tucker didn't know about them as Tucker rarely knew about anything. She herself found out by accident. She was talking to some horny married guy in the home office who thought he was God's gift to women. He was the typical male jerk. He thought he was some type of sex god so he let it slip that there would be another round of layoffs. He was simply trying to impress her. He actually thought she would now drop everything, hop on a plane, fly out to meet him and get laid. Men were so dumb. The truth of the matter was if she did do that, the poor guy would literally die. That would make the trip worthwhile but a good waste of an airfare.

"All I know there is going to be cut backs on the West Coast and some scatterings here and there. More automation is coming so they feel they can eliminate more people."

Tucker hated automation. All that meant was that CMI was going to get even more screwed up than it already was. Their goal was to have everyone and everything on line. All the forms, policies, agents, employees, payroll, vendors. *Everything.* They kept updating the system and so far there was no one in the company that understood the system. Tucker knew he didn't, no one in underwriting did, no one in claims did, no one in payroll and none of the clerical did and no one in Insurance Systems (IS) did. CMI was too busy updating the updates before you could even learn what they were updating. So far they had managed to piss off about all of their agents, insureds, vendors and anyone else who had any work connection with CMI.

"How soon?" Tucker asked.

"I think soon." Vicki would have gotten the date but talking to that sleaze ball made her feel ill so she told the horny goof that she had some work to do and hung up and went back to reading her magazine of the day. She should have reported him, but nothing would have happened. Most men are like that even the ones who think they are not. It was easier to hang up.

"What's Schwartz like?" He asked her. He knew Schwartz somewhat; after all he was a Vice President of something. But Tucker always made it a policy not to get too close to those idiots. They were always talking about bottom line and marketing strategies and all the stupid corporate shit they think is so important.

"David?"

Jesus, she is on a first basis with him. "Yeah, David."

"Typical corporate Home Office ass, why?"

"He wants to pay us a visit in a couple of days and I want to put him off till after Muldoon's dad is buried. Any suggestions?"

"Send him an email. They all like getting email. Makes them feel computer literate."

Tucker left and returned to his office to send an email to Schwartz. He felt that he should let Schwartz know that Muldoon's dad had died and that because of this Schwartz may want to postpone his trip. At least Tucker was hoping he would. He had no intention of going into the Roundtree debacle, as Tucker could not explain it. The Home Office liked explanations. Though they never seemed to have to give any for their idiocy, they expected everyone else to be able to have an explanation for everything all the time. The corporate double standard. Anyway how could he explain South America? He also did not want to tell them about Robinson. As every time a black left it made them nervous. Meant they would have to find a new one somewhere. They liked to showcase the blacks. CMI had very few blacks, very few Hispanics, very few minorities of any type. Diversification was not its strong suit.

Tucker hated writing email but it was better than calling someone and always getting their voice mail. He figured that if he kept it short and sweet it should serve the purpose.

Hi David,

Sorry I missed your call. The reason I am writing is, though we all are looking forward to your visit Larry Muldoon's father passed away in a hospital in Florida while trying to stay healthy. I doubt if Larry will be here to visit with you due to the pending funeral. As you know Larry is looking forward to Omaha but at this time I do not think the time would be good to visit with him.

Perhaps you can reschedule for after the funeral.

Joe Tucker

Tucker read it over twice. Almost made sense so there was a good chance that someone in the home office may actually understand it. Due to the fact that Schwartz was a VP his understanding it would be highly unlikely. Tucker had debated in his own mind whether or not he should say anything about Roundtree or Robinson and decided to hell with it. Why worry about people who weren't here or might not be here at some future date. Anyway Trevayne hadn't yet turned in his resignation and Roundtree, well Roundtree was simply Roundtree. Tucker didn't understand why he simply couldn't take a little nap every day like Phillips, be present but unaccounted for.

EIGHT

Muldoon was traveling on I-294 going south to 95th Street.

Usually when alone in the car he would listen to a sports radio

station but this morning he was not in the mood for their useless

drivel. Exiting off the toll road at 95th He traveled east through Oak

Lawn to the funeral home. .   Going east on 95th Street he

thought he hit every light. He often wondered when he saw that

much traffic just exactly where everyone was going. The wake and

burial would be on the south side. Muldoon's dad was what the

locals called south side Irish. Now there were very few Irish left on

the south side, but once a south sider always a south sider

The year before his parents' retired they bought a condo in Sebring, Florida. Their plan was to go down there each winter, January thru March and spend the rest of the year in their modest bungalow on the south side. But the time spent in Florida kept growing longer and longer till eventually they started going down in early October, coming home for Christmas, then back to Florida and then not returning till the end of April then into May and eventually June. Then they sold their home in Chicago as the cost and aggravation of having two places wasn't worth it and now only came home at Christmas.

They had 12 good years in Florida and now Muldoon wondered what his mother would do. Would she stay in Florida, or return here? Chicago was not the city they left.

None of the family lived in Chicago. All their friends lived in suburbs but told people they lived in Chicago. Then three of her four children didn't even live in Illinois. His mother was independent and still in good health but whether she would want to spend all her time in Florida, alone, without her family remained to be seen. Something to think about now that he and Sarah may be going to Omaha.

He pulled into the parking lot of Dillards Funeral and parked in the back row. He slowly walked to the front door. It was a clear, clean fall day. His car was the only car in the lot. He didn't know if he should take this as a good sign or not. Perhaps no one was dying or if they were dying perhaps they were being buried from somewhere else.

There was a doorbell that Muldoon pushed and immediately was answered by a distinguished looking man in a pin stripe suit, salt and pepper hair, and a funeral directors look of concern and sadness. He was handsome with dark eyes and the smell of Old Spice. "You must be Mr. Muldoon, I am Terry Ford". He extended a hand and Muldoon could see the French cuffs extend from the sleeve of the suit.

He escorted Muldoon into an office located off the main lobby of the building. The inside if the building was spotless. It looked as if the carpet had just been vacuumed. The woodwork all shined as if just polished. The smell of flowers was in the air. There were several oil paintings on the wall. Muldoon noticed them but knew next to nothing about art. As they entered an office Ford pointed to a chair for Muldoon, "Kindly have a seat. Sorry to hear of your loss. Would you like some coffee?" Everything he said sounded sincere. He was probably thru this so many times it was like a recording.

"No Thanks."

"I spoke with your sister this morning. As you know your father's body will be transferred here as soon as it arrives which may even be while we are meeting." He took a seat behind his desk. The desk was neat and orderly. Not like an underwriter's desk thought Muldoon.

Muldoon was somewhat numb. He had never planned a funeral before and wasn't really sure how he was supposed to act. Was he supposed to look and act sad or was he supposed to be very business-like as if he was in complete control? Was he allowed to smile? Should he try to make things upbeat knowing that his dad did not want some sad eyed affair for his send off.

"Are you familiar with our services Mr. Muldoon?"

"You may call me Larry, and no I am not." Why would anyone be familiar with their services Muldoon wondered. Someone died you brought him here; they dressed him, said some prayers and buried him. What is there to be familiar with?

"Your sister said the family would like something simple."

"Whatever simple is." Muldoon said with a smile. He should have known Marie would have covered all the bases.

Ford simply looked at him. Perhaps I shouldn't have smiled Muldoon thought.

"How would you like the death notice worded?"

Muldoon's brain and face went blank. He never thought about a death notice, yet everyone had one.

"Did he have any surviving brothers and sisters?"

Muldoon mentioned his Aunt Helen and his Uncle Jack and his brothers, sisters and the grandkids and some general information.

"Do you want a picture?"

"A picture of what?"

"A picture of your dad in the notice. A lot of people do that now. It is not necessary but some like the thought."

Muldoon didn't know this as he never read the death notices. Now and then he would glance but he can't recall seeing any photos, probably wasn't paying attention. He started to wonder at what age do you have to be before you feel you should be reading the death notices. None of his friends had died, no former schoolmates, but then how would he knew if he never read the notices.

"How about the Internet?" Ford asked.

"What about it?"

"Do you want the notice on line?"

"People read death notices on line?" Muldoon found this very strange.

"Some people move away and like to keep in touch as to what is happening back home."

Muldoon had never read a death notice on line. Seems like a waste of the Internet he thought. *I am going to go on line honey to see if Aunt Martha bought the big one.*

Okay dear and while you are at it check on our old neighbor Harriet Robbins. She should be dead by now.

"It doesn't cost that much more."

Muldoon didn't even want to know what "that much more" was. He said no to the picture in the notice and somehow felt guilty for saying no. Maybe his dad wanted his picture in the paper, but then, not under these circumstances. His dad was dead but he was afraid he would somehow not approve of this decision. He did allow the notice to go on line for he felt that there might be some people in Florida that would be interested in it. He figured that is what they did in Florida, read death notices. Perhaps they would be disappointed that there was no photo.

"Your sister mentioned that you would like the funeral mass to be at St. Thomas the Doubter, his old parish."

Muldoon could only nod. Marie sure could be organized.

"Do you know if you brother will be celebrating the mass?"

Marie had obviously covered all the bases.

"I only know that my brother will be here, whether he has plans to say the mass I don't know." Muldoon was glad he wasn't Frank. That would be a tough decision. May want a few moments to himself instead of up there in front of everyone.

"Your sister said they have a plot in Holy Sepulcher. We will arrange for the grave to be dug and the necessary arrangements to be made there. Would you like to see the caskets?"

"Sure." After the word was out of his mouth he hoped he hadn't sound enthused.

He followed Ford and the scent of Old Spice out of the office down a long corridor past three chapels. All were empty. Muldoon wanted to ask how business was but thought that would be a stupid question. The building was very quiet. Ford opened an oak door at the end of the corridor, which opened to a stairway leading to the second floor. Muldoon followed. At the top of the stairs there was another door that opened to a room full of caskets. He wondered how they got them up here.

"Elevator," as if Ford was reading his thoughts.

There must have been a dozen or so displayed around the perimeter of the room as well as couple towards the center. There were two small caskets there for children Muldoon assumed and seeing them only depressed him.

Ford led Muldoon along the wall describing briefly each casket. They had stainless steel, bronze and copper. They had theme caskets, where you could place a picture of the loved one, or a favorite picture of his, say the skyline of Chicago on the side and top of the casket. If the deceased was a fisherman you could have his fishing polls prominently displayed. Ford mentioned that more and more people were going with a theme. Muldoon didn't understand why you would want a theme at your funeral but only nodded.

Ford made it sound as if some caskets would be more comfortable for the deceased than others. Muldoon could think of no reason why that should be a concern. It was like buying a car. Every casket seemed to have a list of options to choose from.

"Did your father play golf?"

The question surprised Larry, and he had to stop and think a minute. "Well he tried." In fact his dad was a horrible golfer, mainly played golf to drink beer.

"We have this casket here, Larry." Ford said leading Muldoon to an all wood casket that was very impressive. It was highly polished and did look quite comfortable. Muldoon thought perhaps it was mahogany or cherry wood

"A lot of our friends who are involved in sports do like this one." Ford said running his hand along the side of it. "It is mahogany almost like an old time wood driver. Like our other models this has a locking mechanisms and a continuous weld that seals the bottom from moisture and an adjustable bed and mattress.

You will note the rubber seal to keep out the moisture." Ford pointed to the seal so Larry wouldn't miss this feature.

Muldoon noted, and even ran his finger along it. Reached in and felt the mattress. It did feel comfortable. He wanted to know why they had to be locked. Seemed odd. Do the dead try to escape, or are there really grave robbers looking for that gold filling lurking in the shadows. But they all had this feature so he figured it was standard kind of like a radio in car. Finally Muldoon picked out a metal casket called *Peaceful Rest*. Sounded stupid but peaceful. He thought his father would approve. The price was right just under three grand.

"An excellent choice."

Muldoon wondered if he should feel good for making this "excellent choice" then he figured that Ford said this to all the casket buyers.

They returned to the office where final details were worked out. Then Ford asked, "Do you need a vault?"

Once again Larry was dazed and confused, "a vault?"

"For the casket. Casket goes inside the vault. Vault is made of concrete. Keeps the vermin out, insects and the like." While saying this Ford kept writing on a ledger adding up the numbers. "It is not necessary," Ford continued, "but some like the loved one in a safe environment."

"But he is dead."

"I just mention it to let you know that it is available, though not necessary."

"Well I think we can skip that feature." Muldoon told him.

"How did your dad die?" Ford looked up with a show of concern.

"Was in a hospital for a checkup, had a heart attack from what we understand."

"People do die in hospitals," Ford sadly shook his head. "Makes you wonder."

Back in his car he sat in the parking lot wondering if what he did was right. He had not been to that many wakes, and never paid much attention to the caskets or vaults. He simply hoped the one he picked would be okay and everything would go smoothly.

He then cried.

He was alone, and he cried.

He was going to miss his dad. Though his dad spent his later years in Florida simply knowing he was there was a comfort. Now that comfort was gone and he felt that maybe now he would have to be the man of the family. His brother Frank was in Rome across an ocean and busy with saving souls and whatever priests do in Rome and in all honesty did not show that much interest in the family. His brother Tom was busy trying to reach the Majors and get laid as often as possible and was two thirds of a continent away, and his sister was busy ruling her little part of the world from Columbus.

He cried quietly for a few minutes and somehow felt better for having done it. He sat and thought that now it was all out of his hands. His dad was on a plane, the funeral home would pick him up, lay him out. The cemetery plot was there. The church was waiting. Now all everyone had to do was get past the next few days.

He thought of Omaha and what would happen there. It seemed that suddenly things were out of control. He wiped his eyes, took a couple of deep breaths and started the drive home wondering when he would be back in control again.

* * *

Bosco waited for Gladkowski to leave the shop and met him in the office. Bosco was sitting with his back to the door when Gladkowski entered, "Well what brings you here John?"

"Muldoon's father is dead," Bosco smiled.

"Who is Muldoon?" Gladkowski said walking around to his chair behind the desk.

"He is an underwriter for us, as matter of fact a supervisor I think," Bosco wasn't sure. It seemed everyone had a title. "Anyway it is his brother who is the priest in Rome, but now that the old man died the brother will be here for the funeral."

"And?" Gladkowski obviously didn't see the connection.

"I can get the exact price for getting back in the priesthood. The brother will be here and I will be able to talk to him directly. It is as if the Good Lord is watching over me." Bosco told him.

"There is an exact price for this?" Gladkowski asked in wonder.

"There is a price for everything." Bosco said with much confidence. "What do you think you become a Bishop because you know how to pray, or preach a good sermon? That has nothing to do with it. It is how you manage people, money, and know when to shut up and whose ass to kiss and how to raise money. Everything has a price."

"Ain't religion grand?"

"Yep, and if you play it right they might even make you a saint."

"I doubt if that will happen with the present company," Gladkowski said.

"Well you never know." Bosco thought you might be able to buy that as well, if it wasn't for that two miracle rule.

"So how is this going to affect our little deal?" Gladkowski asked.

"Hopefully it won't other than get me the price, and we may have to speed things up."

"What do you want me to do? Have people start running into each other? Anyway you are the guy who is supposed to be sending me the people."

"That won't be a problem, as matter of fact I have one coming your way tomorrow." Bosco had just come from an insured that got rear-ended. Car was still drivable. Trunk and right wheel well damaged. "Guy's name is Sampson, minor damage but easily padded. Give him a loaner and he won't care what you do. The goof that hit him didn't have insurance. We will go thru the motions of going after him, but seeing he is a dead beat, does not believe in speaking English in this great land of ours, but is able to count money I might add." Bosco could never understand how some people supposedly could not speak English, but once you showed them money they became bilingual. "CMI will be stuck."

Gladkowski could only nod in agreement. It was amazing how many people did not have insurance. But as long as there were politicians looking for votes someone would always bail the deadbeats out. And it would always be a politician. Sticking it to the working man was one thing a politician knew how to do.

Gladkowski hated politicians, especially aldermen and ward committeemen. They always had their hands out. When Gladkowski got one of their cars to repair he would always leave something undone. Maybe a loose screw, bolt, nothing major, but something that in time would cause a problem for the guy and being a politician too stupid to trace it back to Gladkowski.

Nothing gave him a grander feeling that fucking over a politician.

"So you, god and this priest are going to get all your ducks in a row at this funeral?" He asked Bosco.

"That is the plan."

"Hope it works."

"It will. I've been praying."

Gladkowski could only roll his eyes to the back of his head. If it wasn't for religion the world would be a nice place to live he thought to himself.

* * *

Dear Mr. Tucker,

As you know I have been with CMI for over 30 years. During this time I have had the pleasure of making many important decisions that helped CMI make lots and lots of money. I believe I was one of the first Blacks ever hired by CMI, and in that 30 years I was always one of the first Blacks to be overlooked for any promotion that came along. In a strange way I am proud of that fact as well. Oh, there were times when I was offered a promotion but it was usually something quite lame and distasteful. You all know what they were. I suppose I could have sued, and won the big bucks, or got the Reverend Jesse Jackson on my side. However, like many whites, I too cannot stand the Reverend Jesse Jackson. I am not a vengeful man and I realize that CMI has given me the opportunity to own my own home, send my kids to college and pay an outlandish price for my daughter's wedding. Therefore now that I am fully vested I be retiring affective the end of this year, December 31.

Sincerely,

Trevayne Robinson, CPCU

CC: Mr. David Schwartz. Vice President

Tucker read it twice. Robinson just couldn't quit. Just couldn't send a short note saying *I quit*. No he had to write a stupid epistle about how being Black he was and is allegedly discriminated against. Smokes were simply a pain in the ass. Anyone else would have just quit, but not Trevayne. Now the do-gooder Schwartz will read it and wonder what the hell is going on. Why did he have to send a copy to Schwartz?

Tucker saved a copy to his computer and printed a copy. He assumed eventually Robinson would hand deliver another one, but to be safe Tucker thought it best to have one on file.

Tucker was starting to be concerned that his office was slowly starting to come apart at the seams. First the idiot Roundtree goes to South America because his son is also an idiot. Robinson quits, which Tucker should have seen coming, but Tucker hated to admit he took Trevayne for granted. For a Black he was dependable, not like that idiot Phillips who spent more time asleep than awake. Tucker was going to have to have a talk with him.

Then there was the Bernie factor, another idiot. Then there is the idiot Father Bosco. Wanted to become a priest again but first his divorce had to be finalized, then his annulment go through and then the Church let him back in. How could he explain that to anyone? If that happened they would need a new Claims Manager, which could mean more interviews. More lying resumes to read. Where would it end?

Then there was Muldoon. Having Muldoon go to Omaha now might not be a good idea. He would need at least one person in the office that knew what was going on. True there was Doris, but lesbians can get funny. Queers all think the world owes them a living for being queer. It should be the other way around; they should owe us the living for putting up with their nonsense. But they got the media behind them who for reasons unknown to Tucker feel we should be tolerant of everyone all the time. The thin-skinned media always making the rules for everyone else, but never following the rules they set. Tucker was convinced if you walked thru any newsroom in America there would be a token Black, a token Hispanic and everyone would be straight.

Now David Schwartz was coming to town. Tucker tried to put it off telling him about Muldoon's old man but Schwartz felt he couldn't change the trip now. People die he told Tucker and life must go on. Sounded like corporate stupidity to Tucker. Common sense would be to wait till Muldoon's dad was buried and Muldoon was back to work. People don't think I have common sense he thought to himself. Compared to the corporate idiots above him he had more sense in a fingernail on his left hand than they had in their entire bodies. Now he would get Robinson's email and have more questions for Tucker.

He fingered his lobe. Too late to do anything about that, but then perhaps before Schwartz arrives a piercing wouldn't hurt.

Maybe he could move Schwartz's trip back a day or two after all some of the office would go to the funeral, out of respect for Muldoon. Hell, Larry was a well liked guy, his old man was as Irish as Paddy's pig, and probably be a meal afterwards. Tucker was definitely going to go. He would simply send off an email to Schwartz. Nice thing about email you didn't have to talk to anyone.

If Schwartz saw it in black and white he would come to his senses and delay everything at least 24 hours. Fingering a lobe Tucker turned to his computer and saw he had an email from Schwartz.

Tucker didn't want to open it but he knew he would have to eventually. It was like a trip to a dentist, opening an email from a suit.

Joe,

Have Trevayne's email. Sorry to see him go. We will have to find a new one.

Call a headhunter to see if they know of someone looking for work that will fit our system. I checked my schedule and I should be arriving Thursday AM. I will simply meet you in the office as I will be staying in the Loop and will walk over. We will meet on Thursday then with everyone hopefully on Friday. Or we could make it Saturday if anyone there works on Saturday.

Have a good day

David

All Tucker could think was shit, shit, shit. *Have a good day.* What a crock. *Call a headhunter. We will need to find a new one.* How did this guy become a VP of anything? He is dumber than me.

NINE

Marie and Emily looked tired. Muldoon met them at O'Hare. Their plane arrived around 6:30 that night. Marie was all business getting the luggage while Muldoon stayed with his mother. Emily didn't say much. Muldoon consoled his mother as best he could but there was not much he could say. . She seemed to be okay other than for the fatigue. When they got to the house Sarah had made some ham sandwiches. They ate and his mother wanted to lie down. Sarah took her to her room and helped her unpack and get settled in. Sarah did this thinking that Larry and Marie would want to be alone with their thoughts and memories.

Larry was in the kitchen with Marie. She looked older for some reason. She recently turned 40 but she looked older. Muldoon blamed it on the travel. She was wearing jeans and a blouse and most of her make-up was worn from the long day of travel.

"Do you know what happened?" She asked him.

All Muldoon could think was, what now?

"There was no priest there."

"Where?"

"When he died. Mom noticed it right away. She is really aggravated by it."

Larry had nothing to say simply shrugged his shoulders.

"You know we were told all thru school that if you made the nine First Fridays you will have a Happy Death. A priest would be there. That is a promise the Church made to get you to go to mass on the First Friday of every month."

"They lied." He told her. Muldoon's theory was simple. Organized religions had to lie to make things sound good or no one would join up. Made no difference what the religion was, just the way it was.

"Well she is going to come down on Frank." She took a drink from her coffee. Set the cup down and reached for the sugar bowl and put a bit more in. "She feels that she and dad made the nine First Fridays probably one hundred times and that should have guaranteed a priest. We both know they played by all the rules."

Muldoon was speechless.

"Well they can't be everywhere." He finally said.

"Should have been in Fort Myers," she paused, "You know I think she is right. They want your money. They want your time. They want you to do this and to do that. They make promises to you, and repeat them over and over and over so you feel that beyond all doubt the promises will be kept and then they're not. And the older you get the more religious you become, and you expect your debts to be repaid."

"Well a priest might not have made any difference," he said. Their dad led a pretty simple life. Stayed married to one woman didn't cheat, didn't swear, steal or kill. Went to church, gave to charities as long as they made sense, and minded his own business. Priests should be so good.

"That is not the point. Martin Luther raised hell when the Church sold indulgences this is just as idiotic."

Muldoon wanted to change the subject to anything but religion as it sounded as if she was ready to start another Reformation. He was tempted to tell her about Bosco but didn't want to get involved with that idiocy, and with a brother a priest there would be enough religion around to cover all the bases.

"Did the funeral parlor call?" She changed the subject.

"Yeah Dad arrived safe and sound and will be ready for viewing tomorrow afternoon. The Death Notice will be in the paper starting tomorrow."

Marie seemed distracted looking here and there. Not seeming to stay focused.

Sarah returned. She looked to Larry, "She is lying down. I think if she can get some rest it will help her for tomorrow."

She turned to Marie, "You too look tired, feel free to lie down any time you want. You don't have to stay up with us."

"Marie says he didn't have a priest." Muldoon didn't even know why he said it.

"I'm sure it won't make any difference. He was a good man and I doubt if a priest would have made any difference." Sarah could always make things sound simple and easy at times.

"A promise made is a debt unpaid," Marie said.

Sarah recognized it as a line from the poem *The Cremation of Sam McGee* by Robert W. Service. *A promise made is a debt unpaid, and the trail has its own stern code.* Sarah didn't realize that Marie knew poetry. Robert W. Service was one of Sarah's favorites.

"Is Harry here yet?" He asked his sister.

She looked at Larry then Sarah, let out a sigh, "We're separated. He moved out about a month ago." Tears came to her eyes. "Everything is going sour at once."

Sarah went over to her and gave her a hug. Muldoon just stood there surprised. Making the nine First Fridays and not having a priest show up was one thing but a divorce that was like a death sentence to the Church. And this would be worst news for his mother than the fraud of the Nine First Fridays. Her generation simply didn't believe in divorce. When you got married you stay married. Kind of like joining the Mob.

It was one of those things that surprised you but then at the same time it really didn't. Harry was an okay guy, somewhat anal, but then he was a college professor and sort of out of touch with real world. Still he looked at his sister and said, "Christ, what happened?" He found it hard to believe that his sister, the rock of the family, would have a failed marriage.

"I don't know. I think we are just getting sick of each other."

"Does Mom know?"

"God no," she sobbed. I don't have the heart to tell her, especially now, and with Frank coming," she wiped her eyes, "I just don't know. And the church doesn't like people who get divorced." She sounded frustrated, angry and scared.

"They don't really like much of anything." He told her hoping it would be a comfort.

Muldoon was going to tell her they were thinking of moving to Omaha as he thought it sounded like something positive. But with his dad dead, and his mother mad at the Church, Marie separated, frustrated and angry and Frank on his way it seemed like he and Sarah's little lives were pretty insignificant.

Sarah said, "Things have a way of working themselves out."

"Is Harry coming to the Funeral?" He asked again.

"Yeah, he will be here. He is not that cruel. It is just something that happened. It is hard to explain. I can't believe I am telling you. You and Sarah are lucky don't screw it up."

It was directed to him and not Sarah. He thought if things did get screwed up that it could be Sarah. After all it took two to tango, and it would take two to screw things up. He figured that when Harry arrived he would be blaming Marie. But he kept that thought to himself.

"Why don't you lie down," Sarah suggested. "It has been a long day for you. Just try to get a good night's sleep and you will feel better in the morning."

Marie seemed to agree with Sarah and slowly got up from the table. She gave them both a hug before making her way to bed.

Muldoon had never hugged his sister so much in his life as he did today.

Sarah gave Larry a kiss and hug and she too went off to bed. Larry was alone in the kitchen. He walked over to the refrigerator and took out a beer and walked outside to the deck. The night was cool and clear.

The World Series was going on but no one seemed to be paying attention. Yankees against the Dodgers but no one cared. When he was a kid he couldn't wait for the World Series, now it was just another TV show with too many commercials. Somewhere along the line something got out of whack and his interest faded. His dad was a big fan, but he said once they starting playing the World Series at night, that was the beginning of the end. Took all the fun out of it. Money cannot replace fun his dad had told him. Looked like his dad had been right.

He took a drink from the can, set it down on the deck rail, and looked up. He could see the stars. If he had any knowledge of the galaxy he would recognize the constellations, but he didn't. It was kind of like not recognizing that his sister was in a marriage that was not working. But then she was in Ohio and he was here, so how would he have known?

He and Sarah were pretty lucky. They didn't have a lot of problems. He assumed there were times they were sick of each other, but there were more times when they seemed to enjoy being together. At least he did. Larry always felt that the reason for divorce was most people simply gave up. Easier to quit and walk away then to make it work. True, if you hated someone no point sticking around, but it was like Marie said, they were getting tired of each other, which is a lot different than hating each other.

He hadn't had much of a chance to talk with his mother. She was tired and he hoped she was sleeping. He didn't know what she would do now that his dad was gone. If she wanted to move back he supposed they could make room for her, or perhaps she would want her own place. He didn't think she would want to go to Columbus, and when she heard about the separation she would only become angry and Marie wouldn't want her there.

He thought of Omaha, but now that seemed to be turning into a blur. He couldn't focus on it. Everything seemed to be happening at once.

Frank and Tom would be here by morning, if not here already. Frank was walking into a buzz saw. No priest at his dad's bedside. His sister getting divorced. The Bosco fiasco. Frank would get an ear full on that. Tom would simply laugh it all off.

Suddenly the thought came to him that he lived in a strange family. His mother was mad at the Church for having lied to her. Frank was a priest in that Church who may try to defend the lie. His sister was in a failing marriage. Tom was sleeping his way thru Triple A baseball. And he didn't really know where he and Sarah would be living a year from now.

He wondered what his dad would think of it all. Probably shrug and figure somehow it would all work out and life would go on. He would probably be pissed about not having a priest at his deathbed. He would assume that Harry and Marie would work things out. If worse came to worst it would be some type of amicable parting. The old man wasn't that fond of Harry to begin with. He got sick of Harry within a year, probably wonder why it took Marie so long. He was proud of his son Frank being a priest and assigned to Rome. Though no one actually knew what he did in Rome it sounded impressive, *my son is a priest in Rome. I think he hears the Pope's confession.* People assumed Frank was on a first name basis with the Pope. Tom being an umpire would make him think back to the days when baseball was fun, the fun he had playing it, watching it, and arguing about it.

What would his dad he think about me, Larry wondered? Be proud that I had both feet on the ground, or more proud that I married Sarah and she saw to it that I kept both feet on the ground.

He took a long drink from his beer and emptied it and went back inside. The house was quiet. He checked the doors out of habit, turned off the light in the kitchen and then laid in bed for two hours staring at the ceiling alone with his thoughts.

TEN

I have often heard the story
But I never told the tale
That even when you're right
You can sometimes fail

I never knew the music
But I always knew the tune
November is a lousy month
And sometimes so is June

I never played the game
But I always knew the score
Sometimes wanting less
Is the same as wanting more.

I never learned to run
But I could always walk
Never learned to speak
But I could always talk

I never learned to sit
But I could always stand

Never liked to clap
But I can give you a hand

You try real hard to win
To have no loss just gain
But that is hard to do
Living life in the slow Lane

Sarah couldn't sleep. It was 5:30AM and she was sitting at her desk in the basement writing. She had been up for about 45 minutes. It was unusual for her not to sleep. She usually slept like a baby. But too much was going on around her. Just the other day they were thinking of moving to Omaha, but now that seemed like years ago. Now Larry's dad is dead. His sister and mother are upstairs sleeping. Even Larry managed to fall asleep. She would fall asleep then awaken. She repeated this process over and over till finally she decided the hell with it. She got up and looked in on the kids, made some coffee and made her way to her little corner of the world.

She looked at her poem and figured it was simply drivel. But then drivel usually made money. She heard footsteps on the stairs behind her turned and saw Marie coming down the stairs. She looked alert for so early in the morning.

"I thought I heard you down here," Marie said.

"How did you sleep?" Sarah asked.

"Better than I thought I would. I'm kind of lucky I don't need much sleep." She set down a coffee cup on the edge of Sarah's desk and grabbed a card table chair that was nearby and slid it over. "You're up early."

Sarah let out a sigh. "I woke up and couldn't get back to sleep. So came down here. I am sorry to hear about you and Harry." She added somewhat hesitantly.

"It's okay" Marie sighed. "At one time I thought being a professor's wife might lead to something like this. Being at Ohio State I thought someday maybe he would become enthralled with a co-ed as those things do happen. But he went and found someone on the Internet."

"The Internet!" It was almost a shriek. Sarah couldn't believe what she heard.

"Yeah, it is like he is a kid again so damn stupid it is unbelievable. He was in a chat room supposedly discussing current

217

events. Met by chance, so he says. They hit it off. She is 29 years old. Lives in Sandusky, which made it real convenient. Basically up the road. They exchanged photos and one thing led to another." Marie reached for her cup not believing she was telling this all to Sarah. But then she felt good for having someone to tell. It was like a release of some type.

"How do you know all this?"

"He is so damn stupid he told me. He likes to think he is Mr. Open Minded. Sometimes I can't believe he is a professor. If Cheerios were brains he'd be General Mills." Marie set the cup on the desk and stood and stretched.

Sarah noticed that Marie seemed more relaxed not as down as she appeared yesterday. "So what do you think will happen?" Sarah said.

"I don't know," she shrugged. "He thinks he wants a divorce. He is supposedly in love with her. Her name is Becky, Jesus Christ, a Becky. I said 'I thought you were in love with me and the kids?' He tells me he is but he needs to expand his horizons. He comes up with all the bullshit right out of the blue."

"Kind of young for him, isn't she?"

"I'm sure that is part of the attraction. He probably thinks he's some kind of stud."

"How do you meet on the Internet?' Sarah was having trouble comprehending that part. "You type little notes to each other and fall in love?'

"I guess," Marie shrugged "People do it. I've heard of it. So I guess it happens." Then she thought for a minute, "Hell I know it happens," And let out a smile.

"You seem to be taking it well all of a sudden."

Marie got up and was walking around the basement with nervous energy. "At first I couldn't believe it. I was ashamed kept asking myself 'where did I go wrong". You know all the guilt trips, blaming myself.

"Then about a week or so ago I thought to myself, I've been a good wife, a good mother, a good person, screw him. I decided that I was going to hang the bastard. Go for the gold. Throw caution to the wind. The whole nine yards.

"Then dad died and I had second thoughts. It felt like everything was coming apart at the seams. But then when I told everyone yesterday, I felt a relief. So I am back in the hanging mode. Anyway I know my dad would want me to hang him."

"Maybe he will get over it and come to his senses."

"He is thinking with his dick, and I am thinking with my brain. So I'll win. If he can think with his dick then I'll fuck with his brain."

That made Sarah smile, "If there is anything Larry and I can do just ask."

"You have your own life. The tough part will be telling my mother."

"You don't have to. You can wait." Sarah suggested.

"She always has a way of knowing when something is wrong. She'll sense it once Harry shows up if not sooner."

"If you need someone to lean on, you can use me."

Marie knew that Sarah meant it, "Thanks, if it comes to that I will. Actually I am starting to look forward to it just got to keep my composure."

"Kids know?"

"Yeah, Mr. Open Minded told them." Then Marie changed the subject, "what do you do down here so early in the morning?"

Her poem was there for all to see. Sarah at times was shy about sharing her writings. She has shown them to Larry, and sent them off. But that was still an anonymous type operation. Just send them off and sign your name and give them your address in case they want to make you rich. "I do some writing. It seems to help relax me."

"What kind?

"Poems."

"Really." Marie sounded somewhat surprised. "Can I read it."

Sarah gathered the paper and handed it to Marie. "Now this is not great poetry, it is just something I like to do."

Marie took the papers, took a sip from her coffee then read. A smile came over her when she finished reading. "This is not bad. Not Byron or Shelley but it has a nice lilt to it." She handed the paper back, "I should do something like this. I could write about my divorce. I was an English Major, and it might help me get through. See how open minded Mr. Open Minded is when I start writing about his foolishness."

They heard some rumblings coming from upstairs and decided they should go up and start breakfast. But before they did they automatically gave each other a hug. They had bonded.

They scrambled some eggs with ham and made some toast. Larry was over at the coffeepot and his mother had just come into the kitchen and sat at the table across from her daughter, Marie. Larry placed a cup of coffee in front of her.

"So what is wrong with you and Harry?" She asked Marie.

Larry shot a quick look at Sarah who simply shook her head no, as if to say, don't get involved.

Marie didn't say anything at first, simply looked at her mother. She didn't want to lie and she knew her mother could put two and two together as well as anyone. "We are separated and talking of divorce."

Her mother looked at her with sad eyes. "The Church is against divorce you know." She let out a sigh, "course they taught that the Nine First Fridays were good for a priest. So I doubt if they got divorce right either."

"You cannot be serious."

Gladkowski had heard it all before. No one believed his estimates. Though this one was padded it wasn't that bad. He had just got through talking with Sampson the guy who got hit by the uninsured motorist, and looking over his car. Bosco's first sucker, so to speak. The damage was confined to the right rear bumper and wheel well, and would need some paint. "Well $5,875 is a good price." Gladkowski told him. Actually $3,150 would have been a better one.

"How the hell can that little dink be that much?" Sampson was a stout guy about five feet eleven who weighed about 225. He had dark greasy hair that he slicked back and horned rim glasses, a Jewish nose and attitude.

Gladkowski figured he suffered from the some kind of Jew complex. Liked to push his weight around. No one was going to push Mr. Jew around.

"Original parts cost a lot of money," Gladkowski told him, though they wouldn't use any on this car as Sampson was proving to be a pain in the ass. He acted like it was his money, which technically it was, but no need to act that way. Jews always pushy.

"Then there is labor costs," Gladkowski continued. "Health costs, taxes, insurance, equipment plus all the environmental bullshit we have to deal with. Sad to say Mr. Sampson this all adds up. The government does not care about the little man. They live to shit on us."

"It's a fuckin' dink."

"Dinks cost money. Here is the printout." Gladkowski handed Sampson a computer printout describing the damage. A work of fiction but a very detailed work and nothing anyone would be able to understand. And a computer printout always made things seem almost official.

"This is bullshit."

"Look it," Gladkowski was starting to lose his patience. "I can't help it. No one believes this stuff. A car is more expensive piece by piece than on the assembly line. I don't understand it, but that's the way it is. And you want to know who to blame. Not me trying to make a buck." He pauses and looks at Sampson. "It is these goddam insurance companies and the politicians. They are out to get the little guy." He said it in such a way he want to think he and Sampson were allies in the quest to save the little guy..

Gladkowski had no idea where he was heading but he kept right on talking, dazzle them with confusion. "Ten years ago I could have fixed this car for under $2,000, but now with all the regulations, laws, directives and OSHA shit I will be lucky to break even on this damn thing.

"And you want to know why? The lawmakers in this country that's why. They hate our guts. You can take that to the bank Mr. Sampson." He waves his finger in the air for emphasis.

"It's bullshit." Sampson said. "A dink shouldn't cost this month."

Gladkowski wanted to cold cock the bastard right in his Jew nose but instead he saved the best for last. "Mr. Sampson," Gladkowski said in a very sincere voice, "CMI recommended us because we are honest and will do a good job for you. And not only that we provide you with a loaner."

"If they raise my rates there is going to be hell to pay."

"We should have your car fixed by Monday, if we can get it done sooner we will." There was absolutely no chance of that

225

happening. Gladkowski would not go out of his way for anyone that complained. It was a company policy.

* * *

Tucker was feeling good. He had another email from Schwartz. The suit was now going to wait till Monday to have his little meeting. Finely dawned on the moron that waiting till after the funeral would work out best for all.

Tucker thought of taking a walk around the Loop to kind of blow off the day, as there wasn't much for him to do. Roam up to North Michigan Avenue, or maybe wander over to Billy Goats have a beer and a burger. Roundtree was still missing in action. Robinson might as well be missing in action. Once someone gave their notice they were pretty much history. Robinson would hang around till the end of the year, and then he could start his retirement with 4 weeks paid vacation. From now till the end of the year he would only be here physically, not mentally.

Too bad they played the World Series at night otherwise Robinson could sneak away in the afternoon to watch it thought

226

Tucker. Even Tucker watched some of the game last night; it was 2-2 when Tucker fell asleep in front of the TV. When he awoke the game was over and some dumb movie was on. He went to bed not knowing the final score, but he did find out this morning that the Dodgers won 7-4.

Tucker knew he should talk to Phillips about sleeping the afternoons away. Being short of help and now with Muldoon gone for the remainder of the week only Phillips and Doris would be doing the work, basically Doris. He figured he would talk to Phillips then take his walk around the Loop.

He didn't want to talk to Phillips, as it could involve making a decision of some type. Something he hated doing but he knew with the office slowly going to hell he should try to get the guy somewhat on board. Then after his talk with Phillips he would wander over to North Michigan Avenue and check out the women.

He walked over to Phillips cubicle mainly to walk by the luscious Vicki's cubicle so he could look in on her to see how she looked and smelled this fine fall day. She was sitting at her desk paging through a catalogue. She looked up and gave him a short smile and he smiled back. He wondered briefly who would be the lucky guy who would get to marry and bed that on a regular basis. But before his mind could wander too far he arrived at Phillip's cubicle.

Phillips was his desk, awake, but not moving. He looked like he was about to doze off. "You awake?"

Phillips moved with a jerk, "of course," he blurted out.

"I would like to see you in my office." He could talk to Phillips here but by having Phillips come to his office he could walk by Vicki's cubicle again.

She was still paging through the catalogue and noticed him slow down and stare in at her. She watched from the corner of her eye as he slowed, took a deep breath, let out a short sigh and continued on his way. What a jerk she thought.

"You called." It was Phillips

Phillips was 48 years old, looked 60. Thinning hair, glasses, his body oval shaped more like an egg than a human. Tucker was almost glad he slept away the days as he didn't like looking at him, "Bad news Fred."

Phillips simply looked no reply.

"Nap time is over. We need you to do some work. I know that may be an appalling concept to you but you are needed."

"For how long?"

"For as long as it takes."

"For as long as what takes?

"The work to get done."

"Doesn't it get done now?"

"Things have changed."

"Like what?"

"Well Roundtree is in South America for starters."

"Not my fault. He could have simply killed the kid."

"Then he would have blood on his hands."

"But the kids wants to be a lawyer."

"Hence, South America." Tucker turned and looked out the window. "Then there is Robinson. He'll be retiring at the end of the year."

"What does that have to with now?"

"You know once you give your notice to hang it up you just coast till the final day."

"I thought that is what white people did. I thought blacks gave their all till the bitter end. That a black would never duplicate what a white man does. Supposedly beneath them, acting white."

"Write a letter to the Reverend Jackson. Sounds stupid enough he might like it. I am sure Jesse will set him straight." Tucker turned back around. "Then there is the Muldoon tragedy. Old man killed by a hospital, the wake, the funeral. So he won't be back till Monday."

"If Muldoon is as efficient as everyone says he would have planned ahead for this day."

"Didn't plan on the hospital attack. Many people miss that."

"If I have to work in the afternoons I am not coming in on Saturdays."

"Do you now?"

"Mainly to rest up."

"I'm counting on you Fred. All it means is about 3 to 4 more hours a day trying to stay somewhat alert."

"What about Doris?"

"She is always alert."

"Rather scary now that you mention it."

Tucker had to agree with that.

"By the way Schwartz is going to be here Monday w

ants to meet with all the underwriters."

"Is he queer?"

"More odd than queer."

"Queers can be odd."

"But they think they're normal."

"That's what makes them odd."

He watched Phillips return to his cubicle taking the detour past Vicki's. He then got ready to take his walk around the Loop. Maybe he would get an earring. But then again he married well and probably wouldn't need one.

ELEVEN

The time arrived to leave for the funeral home. Muldoon was

going to drive with his mother and his sister. Sarah would take the van with the kids. Earlier his mother had read the death notice and thought there should have been more, but more of what she never said. "It is hard to believe you can have your life summed up in about five sentences."

His mother wanted to get to the funeral home before 4PM so she could simply have some time before people started arriving.

The ride was uneventful. The traffic on the toll way was heavy as the toll road is always under construction, "how do you put up with all this traffic?"

Muldoon could only shrug. He didn't know how he put up with all the traffic it simply becomes a way of life. There was no other conversation. The three of them were alone with their thoughts.

Neither Frank nor Tom had put in an appearance but they did know Frank was in town and he would meet them at the funeral home. Tom they assumed would eventually show up. "You would think he would let us know where he was," his mother said more than once.

The traffic going east on 95th Street was as bad as the toll way. Traffic pulling in and out of the numerous strip malls, stores and side streets along the way. People yakking on cell phones while attempting to drive and screwing traffic up even more. Who the hell are they talking to? Then to make matters worse Muldoon hit every red light. He came to the conclusion that no one stayed home for any reason anymore. They were always on the way to somewhere or returning from somewhere. Never at home.

Marie spent the trip sitting quietly in the back looking out the window. Muldoon would glance at her every now and then in the rear view mirror and she had the look of someone who wanted to be left alone. She appeared to be in deep thought.

At ten to four he pulled into the parking lot. He parked where he did on his first visit and the three of them slowly made their way to the front door. Mr. Ford came out of his office to greet them. Larry introduced his mother and sister to him. Ford pointed out the parlor where his dad was, the center one, and if they needed anything, anything at all, just simply ask.

Ford then escorted them to the parlor and let them enter and be alone. Once he was gone Emily said, "He has very sympathetic eyes."

Muldoon barely heard her. He was concerned about how he was going to feel looking at his dad in the casket he had picked for him. How his mother would hold up, and what Marie was thinking.

They approached the casket slowly Marie and Larry on either side of their mother as if they thought she may faint upon seeing her husband.

"He looks asleep," Marie said

"He never dressed that well when he slept." Emily said. She walked to the side of the casket and looked in and touched her husband, "I always hated that tie. I should have burned it when I had the chance." She then knelt at the kneeler, blessed herself and said a prayer.

Larry and Marie stood behind her as she prayed and Muldoon eyes went to the tie, looked okay to him. It was maroon with some little white circles dispersed thru it. Kind of went nice with the blue suit Muldoon thought.

Emily got up and walked over to her children and took Muldoon's arm and simply said, "He was a good man."

Larry and Marie nodded their agreement. Marie took out a handkerchief and wiped her eyes and then walked to the kneeler to say her prayer. His mother walked over to some flowers that were located next to the casket and read the cards. Muldoon noticed that there were flowers on both sides of the casket. He then looked around the room and noticed that it was set up like a theater. All the seating faced the casket. The front row was assorted couches and living room type chairs. Behind them were 10 rows of folding chairs, all padded, and all looking new. The perimeter of the room had assorted pieces of furniture along the walls, chairs, tables, and lamps. It did look somewhat like a parlor.

His mother walked over to him, "You see the flowers over there on the end, the yellow ones?" She asked.

He nodded.

"They are from the people he worked for. He hated those people, forcing him out before he was ready to go. Now they send him flowers. If they had any decency they would have done something for him while he was alive." She went back to looking at the other flowers.

"Mom is holding up well." Marie said.

"She was always strong." Muldoon then walked to the kneeler and knelt and prayed for his dad.

When he got up from his prayer Sarah and the kids walked in. This was the first wake for their kids, and they looked somber and concerned. Their grandmother walked over and gave them a hug and they all walked to the kneeler and said a prayer together.

Mr. and Mrs. Armstrong were the first non-family members to pay their respects. They were neighbors prior to Florida.

"My Larry you look wonderful," Mrs. Armstrong said, "So sorry about your dad. Are these your kids?" She said nodding to the twins and Emily. "They are so big."

Larry introduced his kids.

"She is named after her grandmother how nice."

The late afternoon continued in that manner for the first hour or two and then Tom arrived with a woman, a very good looking woman.

* * *

Gladkowski looked at Bosco and told him, "This Sampson you sent over is going to end up causing us nothing but grief."

"Some guys feel like they have to throw their weight around."

"Yeah, but he is a Jew. They all have a bug up their ass. Spend their free time trying to convince everyone they are big shits like we all should give a shit. "

"But they always end up little turds."

"Keep an eye on him," Gladkowski warned, "He could be a problem.

"I have another one coming in tomorrow." Bosco said ignoring the advice, "Same deal. Guy who hit her had no insurance."

"A woman? She ain't a whiner is she?" Gladkowski hated women that whined. *My husband usually takes care of these things but he is at work. Can I get a ride home? Can you watch my kids? Kind of messy in here.*

"Nah, some divorced woman, kids are grown, she is about 55 or so. Some Smoke plowed into her on the Dan Ryan. Naturally he didn't have insurance. Has money for a Lincoln Navigator but he can't *'for no 'surance."*

"They never think they will have an accident and someone will bail them out."

"Natalie, that is the woman's name, she was simply glad to get out of there alive. Though Tyrone Jefferson Abraham Lincoln, which is also his real name, was going to do her right there on the 79th Street off ramp."

Gladkowski at times found it hard to believe that Bosco was a priest and may very well be one again, as Bosco seemed more prejudiced than Gladkowski and Gladkowski hardly liked anyone

"When did you promise Sampson his car?" Bosco asked.

"You know," Gladkowski said ignoring the question. "Years ago Lincoln Park Zoo had a gorilla they called Sampson, no wait a minute it was Bushman, yeah that was it, Bushman. Anyway it died. I kind of remember it vaguely. But all the newspapers carried on like the President died, and it was just a fuckin' ape." Then Gladkowski added, "For a second I thought Sampson may have been named after a gorilla."

"No, first name is Ira."

"That pretty much guarantees it and an overweight Jew to at that."

"Just give him a sympathetic ear."

"Right, I am sure that will work."

"When is he going to pick up the car?"

"I told him Monday, but since he is obnoxious and a pain in the ass, probably Tuesday or Wednesday.

"Don't jerk him around."

"It's a diversion. You give them something meaningless to be upset about and they forget the real problem, like how they are being scammed on the repair work."

Bosco thought that almost made sense. "You going to the wake?"

"What wake?"

"Muldoon's dad."

"I don't know this Muldoon, or his dead dad. Why would I go to the wake?"

"To get to know the players."

Gladkowski could only look at him with a blank stare. That was one of the dumbest things Gladkowski had ever heard. *To know the players.* "I don't want to know the players. And I sure the hell don't want to go to a wake for some guy I don't even remotely know."

"Yeah, but you could get to meet Frank."

"Who is Frank?

"Muldoon's brother. The priest from Rome. The guy who is going to grease the skids so I can back in the Church's good graces."

All Gladkowski could think was that organized religion was one of the world's great scams. "I'll take the chance that you will be able to handle the chores of mourning for the dead of our little adventure and I will take care of the accident victims"

Just then a tow truck pulled into the lot. "Ah Natalie's car."

"Why didn't you send it over to the East Side since it happened over that way."

"She lives out here, and this would be more convenient for her. Make it easier for the customer and all." Bosco smiled.

"Aren't you the considerate one."

"I try. Well I have a wake to get to. Wish me luck. You may, if you like, want to say a prayer for me."

"What prayer would that be?"

*   *   *

Tom gave his mother a hug and introduced the woman he was with to her. Both women gave each other a warm smile as if they had known each other forever. She was an attractive brunette who looked both athletic and smart.

Muldoon wondered what she was doing with Tom. Muldoon was going to walk over but he thought he would let his brother have some time alone at the coffin and with their mother.

Sarah walked over to Larry, "who is that with your brother? Quite the looker."

Muldoon had noticed that. "Yes, she does look nice."

Tom then saw Larry and Sarah and walked over to them. Tom looked sad but at the same time relieved that he saw someone he knew. He shook his brother's hand and gave Sarah a hug then turned, "this is Cindy, my fiancée."

Both Larry and Sarah were taken by surprise, "Really?" Was all Muldoon could mutter.

"Why congratulations," said Sarah. She was faster on her feet then her husband.

"We plan to get married in Vegas next month."

Holy Shit was all Muldoon could think. Marie getting divorced, his mother mad about the Nine First Fridays, a non-church wedding for Tom and Bosco probably waiting in the wings somewhere. No wonder Frank had yet to show up.

"How nice," said Sarah.

Larry turned and looked at Cindy. God she was pretty. Dark hair, bluish green eyes, not overly made up, an easy smile. She smiled at him and said, "We hope you two can make it."

"Cindy is from Paradise."

"That is obvious, but where is she really from?"

"You are very flattering," Cindy said, "but it is Paradise, California, the northern part of the state, near Chico."

Larry and Sarah nodded as if to imply they knew the geography of northern California.

"Does Mom know you are getting married in Vegas?"

"No. I thought we would wait till after the funeral."

"Well you may want to tell her now as she is pretty down on the Church. Dad didn't have a priest when he died, though he made the Nine First Fridays several hundred times. And Marie is getting divorced."

"Marie is getting divorced, holy shit." Tom turned to Cindy. "Marie is my sister, the heir apparent to my mother." Then he stopped in mid thought and looked to Larry then Sarah then to his mother and back to Larry, "No priest. What kind of bullshit is that? They had us praying our asses off for all kinds of things as kids, and the one thing they counted on they don't get. Well if they weren't off molesting children they could have been there."

"He can get riled up quite easily at times," Cindy told them.

"And what do you do Cindy?" Sarah asked.

"I'm a lawyer."

Tom and Sarah looked at each other *holy shit a lawyer.*

"Tom says a hospital may have killed your dad."

"Well we don't really know that."

Marie then walked over to her brother Tom, "hi stranger" and gave him a hug. Tom made the introductions.

"Cindy is a lawyer." Larry told her.

"Divorce, by chance?"

"I know some very good ones."

"Frank is here."

*   *   *

Tucker skipped his evening cocktail, as he wanted to be alert for the wake. He knew other office members would be there and he wanted to make a good impression and he also wanted to look like a boss. And dozing off from a drink or two at a wake would not leave that impression.

He knew Bosco would be there as the Reverend was going to try to run some scam past Muldoon's brother. Vicki would be there, as would Robinson and Doris and some of the others that Larry came in touch with during the workday.

He also knew Harry Schmidt would be there, as would other agents for CMI.

So Tucker had milk with his supper and a cup of tea afterwards. He was going to be alert, maybe not mentally but at least physically.

TWELVE

Frank looked haggard. There was no mistaking he was a priest, Roman Collar, black suit and scuffed shoes. His mother and Larry spotted him at the same time. Larry wanted to get to him and warn him what might lie ahead for the evening and his mother wanted to get to him to give him hell.

His mother started for him but was interrupted by a mourner who wanted to offer their condolences. Larry got to him first. Frank looked at him and said, "Thanks for Farther Harris. I know I should have stayed in a motel. The man is a nut."

Larry had forgotten about Father Harris and Holy Mother of God Church. Before Larry could respond his mother was there, "we were wondering what happened to you."

He hugged her, "A long flight. Poor connections in New York. How are you doing?"

"Better than your father."

"Since we are all here will you lead us in some prayers?" "She asked.

He walked with her up to where his dad was laid out. The hall was about half full with mourners. Some family, Aunts, Uncles, cousins some old neighbors and old friends his dad and mother had made over the years. Those that recognized him nodded as he walked past and smiled. He hugged Marie and saw Tom off to the side with some babe. He walked to the kneeler, knelt, looked at his dad and starting praying out loud the Our Father. After "who art in heaven" the mourners became quiet and then responded as their Catholic upbringing taught them. After the prayers were recited for the repose of his dad's soul he slowly rose to face his mother

She motioned for him to sit next to her on the small couch she was seated on. Once he was settled she turned to him, "you know your dad didn't have a priest."

"When?"

"When he died, when do you think?" She sounded exasperated, as she couldn't believe he would ask such a stupid question.

He was somewhat dumbfounded. "I never gave it much thought."

"They made the promise."

"Who did?"

"The Church."

He thought he might be suffering from jet lag, as he did not know where this was going. "They promised him a priest?"

"They certainly did."

"Why would they do that?"

"You're the priest," she said. "If anyone should know the rules it's you. He made the Nine First Fridays. He should have had a priest for a happy death, if there is such a thing."

"How did you know he didn't have a happy death?"

"Look it," she said. "When someone makes a promise, and when that someone is the Church, they should keep it. He should have had a priest. We bought into it. Gave money, gave our time. Figuring if we play by the rules we will get a kick-start into heaven. But then The Church just writes us off."

"Maybe he didn't need a priest." He said sounding almost hopeful.

"We are talking about your father," she sounded surprised that he could even think of such a thing, "of course he needed a priest. If you ever played golf with him you know he needed a priest. Then the poor man went into a hospital sinful and healthy and came out dead. Even if they gave him an unhealthy priest in the hospital he would have been better off."

"What do you mean sinful? He was a good man." Frank thought his dad was the salt of the earth. He didn't know a better man.

"Of course he was a good man. But he sinned. Don't tell me he didn't sin. I lived with him for over 45 years. He sinned. And he should have had a priest."

Frank had no response. This was not what he was expecting. He didn't know what he was expecting, but he knew it wasn't this.

"The Church made a promise they didn't keep.' She looked right at him, "Then they wonder why no one goes any more. Well if they are not going to keep their word, why should anyone go? What The Church needs is some women. And not just women priests, but women who are Bishops and Cardinals. They need some women up there calling the shots. But the Church is so afraid of women is it absolutely pathetic. If Christ hadn't risen from the dead He would now be spinning in His grave knowing how wrongful The Church attitude towards women is."

He waited to see if she was finally finished, "Anything else?"

"Mingle and say hello to your sister."

He didn't want to mingle or say hello to anyone, but he did want to meet the woman Tom was with. He may be a priest but he knew a good-looking woman when he saw one.

*   *   *

Muldoon had worked his way to the back of the parlor. At the rear there was an easy chair next to a table with a lamp. Muldoon sat there looking at the backs of the mourners. He didn't know how he was supposed to feel. He only knew that he felt numb. He felt that his mother was taking this all very well. Didn't seem to be upset by her husband's passing, she was more upset that he didn't have a priest with him when he died then the fact that he died.

He watched Frank make his way over to Tom and Cindy. It took Frank some time to reach them as mourners would stop him to shake his hand or give him a hug. The laity liked seeing a priest they knew. One they could identify with, and the fact that Frank was in Rome, *Vatican City*, and probably on a first name basis with the Pope only made it that much better.

"Hi Larry."

Muldoon hadn't seen anyone walk up. He looked to his left and saw Harry, Marie's husband, or maybe the correct term was estranged husband. Muldoon stood to shake Harry's hand and saw Marie and Harry's kids make their way to their mother and grandmother who were both at the front of the parlor

"Hi Harry, how are you?"

Harry looked tired. Bags were forming under his eyes. Probably from the drive. He offered his condolences, "How did he die? Marie never said."

Muldoon told him.

Harry listened and said, "A hospital killed him." He pursed his lips and shook his head, "get a lawyer happens in Ohio all the time."

"Well Tom is dating one now."

Harry turned to the front and saw Tom with Cindy, Frank and Marie. "Is that her?"

"Yeah, the looker"

"Very nice." Harry hesitated, as he knew he should walk up there and offer his condolences. "You hear about me and Marie?"

"She told us yesterday. Sorry". Muldoon never knew if you were supposed to be sorry for people getting divorced. Maybe you should be saying congratulations.

"It's okay. Things happen. Well I should get up and see you mother. Will talk to you later."

Muldoon watched him walk away and thought this would be a long night for Harry, probably a long tomorrow as well. Guess when you make your own bed you got to sleep in it.

"Is the Reverend here?"

It was Tucker he caught Muldoon off guard as he walked up to him from behind. "Reverend Who?" Muldoon responded automatically.

"Bosco, I thought I saw him walk in."

"I haven't seen him, but then I haven't been looking."

"He wants to talk to your brother?"

"My brother may have a full slate tonight." Muldoon could only hope that Tucker wasn't going to be his usual goofy self, but the more Larry thought about it the more he felt that would never happen.

Then they heard the *Our Father* being prayed. Some around them were starting to kneel and respond to the prayer. While others simply took a seat before responding. Muldoon looked to the front to see who it was but he knew who it was, Bosco.

Good God Almighty.

Tucker knelt on the floor next to Muldoon. Muldoon simply stood not believing what he was seeing or hearing. Bosco at the kneeler leading the prayers for the dead. Frank was kneeling and praying not aware that the man leading the prayers was not a priest. His mother was seated and responding. Tucker reached up and tugged on Muldoon's sleeve wanting him to kneel.

"He is not even a priest." Muldoon said.

"Yeah, but these may be the prayers that get your dad into heaven."

Muldoon hadn't thought of that. He knelt and felt that this whole thing was weird.

Trevayne Robinson entered the parlor just as Bosco was starting the first *Hail Mary*. Catholics are always praying their asses off he thought to himself. Robinson was not a Catholic as matter of fact he did not belong to any organized religion. He went to church on Christmas and occasionally Easter. His wife went and those were the one or two days a year he would go with her. She always hoped that he would go more, but he was a good husband, and a good father. He rarely swore, was always there for her so she never made it an issue. She eventually came to the conclusion you can keep the Sabbath holy in more ways than one.

Robinson wasn't going to kneel, as that would be idiotic. He wasn't going to respond either as he didn't really know the *Hail Mary*. He knew the *Our Father* but the Catholics had their own abbreviated version. That was one good thing the Catholics did, they shortened a prayer.

Everyone responded accordingly not realizing that the prayer leader was no longer a priest. That the man leading them in prayer was an ex priest, who got married, getting divorced and hoped to have it all annulled so he could start over. A mind-boggling proposition.

Robinson listened to the prayer and thought the voice sounded familiar. He looked over the shoulder of a man in front of him and saw Bosco at the kneeler next to the coffin. He was wearing a black suit and he was carefully enunciating every word. Robinson thought he would never get done and wondered if anyone could just pop in and start praying. He hoped they weren't expecting it of him. While listening to Bosco's praying he looked around the room and saw Muldoon off to his left and behind him. He was with Tucker. Robinson debated about going over, but he figured it would be the decent thing to do.

Finally Bosco finished. "Quite the pray-er," Robinson said walking up to them and referring to Bosco.

"The Reverend is in fine form tonight," Tucker said.

Robinson shook Muldoon's hand and offered his condolences.

Out of the corner of his eye Muldoon could see Bosco walking over toward Frank Muldoon didn't want to be impolite and simply leave Robinson and Tucker high and dry but then he felt Frank might need some support. "I should introduce my brother to Bosco," Muldoon told them.

"Let us join you," Tucker said. Tucker didn't want to miss this. Muldoon already started walking to the front of the parlor.

Tucker turned to Robinson, "Come on Trevayne this is going to be worth the price of admission."

"Catholics make you pay at these things?" Man no wonder I don't sign up for any of this shit he thought.

"No," Tucker said. "Bosco is going to asked Muldoon's brother about getting back with god."

"You white people be hopeless."

*   *   *

Bosco recognized Muldoon's brother with no trouble. He was the only one there wearing a Roman collar and he looked like Muldoon. He was talking to another guy that could pass for a Muldoon and one hot looking woman. He had no idea who they were.

There was a tug on his sleeve, "thank you," a woman's voice said.

He turned and saw an older woman with kind eyes looking at him, he automatically said "you're welcome", and tried to keep moving towards Muldoon's brother. But she had one hell of a grip. "Can I help you?" He asked in an aggravated manner.

"No. I just want to thank you for praying for my husband."

Now he felt like an idiot. He told himself to calm down. In his anxiety to get to Muldoon's brother he was being rude to Muldoon's mother. Getting back in the Church's good graces was going to tax him. "Oh, I am sorry for your loss, he was a fine man." He said as sincerely as possible.

"Did you know him?'

Ah, shit. He could feel his heart skip a beat what could he tell her? This was getting way too complicated. He didn't know him, never heard of him till he died. How do I get myself in these spots he wondered? Then he saw Larry approaching with Tucker and Robinson.

"You have met the Reverend Bosco," Tucker said to Mrs. Muldoon. Then Tucker introduced himself, offered his condolences.

Bosco could feel the sigh of relief leave his body. He never thought he would ever be happy to come across Joe Tucker.

"I don't recall meeting you," Mrs. Muldoon said to Bosco still impressed by his praying.

"He is a friend of Franks," Larry said.

Then she looked to Trevayne Robinson. Trevayne was a stately presence. Tall, heavy, dark beard neatly trimmed speckled gray in hair and beard. Dark brown suit, crisp white shirt, coordinated tie. She looked up at him with awe and wonder having no idea on who he was or why he would be here. They didn't have any black friends. All their friends were white. As she thought about it she didn't even know anyone black. Everyone was white, and she didn't think any of them had a beard.

"I work with your son Larry," Trevayne told her sensing her bewilderment.

She looked from Trevayne to Larry and back again

"You a Baptist?"

That caught them all of guard, Larry, Bosco and Trevayne. They all looked at each other and back again.

"No I'm not," he finally answered. But then again he thought, maybe he was. He knew his wife attended some church regularly. It could be a Baptist Church. He had been there on Christmas but other than the wailing and the singing and the clapping and the never ending sermonizing he had no idea on what the religion was.

"It's okay. I just thought Blacks were Baptist. It is all right if you're not. Thank you for coming." She patted him on the arm. "My husband would be happy you are here." She then turned to Larry, "have you seen Marie?"

Muldoon looked around and saw Marie in the back of the parlor with her kids and pointed that way for his mother.

"I have something for her," she excused herself and made her way to Marie.

"I got to meet your brother." Bosco was anxious.

Muldoon wanted to tell him that his brother didn't want to be bothered with his stupid drivel, but he knew it would be no use. He led Bosco over to Frank, Tucker and Robinson followed.

Cindy was the first to notice them approach. She smiled and then when her eyes reached Trevayne her eyebrows shot up. It was like she had never seen a big Black man before, well probably never at an Irish Catholic Wake.

"Frank was just telling us if he didn't have a calling he would have been an attorney." She said with a smile.

"Thank god for small favors," Tucker said. "Like we need another attorney."

"I'm an attorney," she told him giving him a cold stare.

Not missing a beat Tucker smiled and said, "But like Frank perhaps you should have been a priest."

"But I'm not a Catholic."

Muldoon instantly thought to himself Tom is marrying a non-Catholic in a non-church wedding. The Church and his mother were going to frown on that combination.

"You are also a woman." Tucker said to her.

"So what?"

"The Catholic Church frowns on women being put in a position where they might actually save a soul."

"That's idiotic," she retorted. "The only soul I am responsible for is my own. What good would it do me to save your soul if I didn't save my own?" From this short conversation she was having with Tucker she could never imagine saving his soul even if the opportunity presented itself.

Tucker never heard it put so succinctly before and for one of the few times in his life did not have a response.

"I don't believe I met your friends," Frank said to his brother trying to avert some the tension that seemed to be building between

Tucker and Cindy. "Are you a priest?" he asked Bosco. He noticed that Bosco was not wearing a collar.

"Yes and no."

"I don't think I understand."

That is not all you are not going to understand Muldoon thought. He then stepped in, "Frank I would like you to meet some of my co-workers." He then introduced everyone including Cindy to the group. Tom had disappeared.

They all shook hands and exchanged pleasantries. "If you have a minute I would like to talk to you alone," Bosco said to Frank.

Frank looked at him and wondered why he wanted to meet alone. Frank then turned to Larry and Larry more or less nodded to his brother that it was okay. Frank then walked over to Larry and said quietly, "Cindy says if we sue the hospital we may have a case."

Muldoon glanced at Cindy. She smiled.

* * *

Trevayne slowly eased his way away for the group. He thought white people were pretty much all nuts, though that Cindy was one nice looking white woman. Trevayne wanted to find Tom, Muldoon's brother, and talk a little baseball and see how he was doing with umpiring. Trevayne didn't know if you were allowed to talk baseball at a Wake, but the World Series was on and it was something to talk about.

Tom was a White Sox fan like Trevayne. They met about three years ago at some CMI function. Why Tom was there Trevayne couldn't recall, but he and Tom hit it off talking baseball and umpiring and Trevayne thought it would now be a way to pass some time. He didn't feel it would be right to simply walk in and walk out, and he knew he didn't want to listen to Tucker and Bosco.

He stood near the back looking around and it dawned on him he was the only black there. The fact that he was the only black was not surprising but the fact that it took him so long to notice it surprised him. People would walk by and pay hardly any attention to him. Some would stare but that seemed to be more due his size than his color. Perhaps that was a good thing he thought to himself. Maybe we all aren't as paranoid as we use to be. But then again he didn't have any white friends, never invited any whites to his home though he worked with many he didn't socialize with them, nor they with him. Muldoon's mother was a bit strange with her Baptist question, but she meant no harm. He remembered when he was the token black at CMI, many years ago. There were more blacks there now, some in good positions. Robinson could have moved up but never did.

Maybe blacks were their own worst enemy trying to find things that just weren't there. Though he would never admit that publicly, the idea that he was thinking that way made him wonder. Maybe whites and blacks aren't as paranoid as the media makes us out to be. He liked Muldoon. Tucker was weird and Bosco was nuts but they didn't harm anyone. The white agents he dealt with were as goofy as the black agents he dealt with, all looking for an angle. And there was the luscious Vicki Higgins. That was one white woman he could really like.

Then on cue the luscious Vicki Higgins entered the parlor. She didn't see Robinson and walked to the front of the parlor where most of the Muldoon family along with Tucker and Bosco were congregated.

She was one good-looking woman and he watched her the entire way. He also noticed the heads of other men in the parlor turn to watch her pass.

Off to the side he saw Muldoon's mother and another woman who he took to be Muldoon's sister in a conversation of some type. Mrs. Muldoon handed the younger woman an envelope. The younger woman frowned, but took it, and said something. The older woman said something back and then they went their separate ways.

He saw Tucker and Bosco talking to Muldoon's brother Frank. Tucker wasn't saying much, looked like he was more or less eavesdropping. Then Vicki arrived at the group and ended whatever conversation they were having.

"The Cubs suck."

Trevayne almost jumped off the floor hearing the voice so entranced was he in watching the luscious Vicki Higgins. It was Larry's brother Tom. They smiled at each other and shook hands. During their visit three years ago they learned that they both hated the Cubs or as their goofy fans call them *the Cubbies*. No true south sider would root for the Cubs under any circumstances. There were some that did but they were misguided and thoughtless and felt by openly rooting for the Cubs they were somehow being open minded. When in truth they were just showing their ignorance.

Trevayne remembered a day some time ago when he was invited by an agent to go to Wrigley Field to see the Cubs play the Giants. He went to see Barry Bonds. All the Cub fans had cell phones and they would call each other *inside the park* and wave to each other and say, "Isn't this awesome". He has never been back, as he doesn't own a cell phone. He thought at the time that to attend a game at Wrigley Field you had to have a cell phone. No one seemed to be there to watch the game; they seemed to be there to use their cell phones. His wife has a cell phone, but he refuses to own one. Under no circumstances does he want to be mistaken for a Cub fan.

"How is umpiring going?" He asked.

"I'm getting there. Going to do some spring training games next spring and could be on my way."

"Sorry about your dad, I know he was a big fan."

"Loved the White Sox. Though he did become disenchanted with the game recently he still followed them."

"Your dad died in a hospital I hear. I only thought that happened to blacks."

"I think we should sue."

"Could have simply been his time. That is what they tell us."

"I don't know, he was perfectly fine, full of life. Goes in for some routine tests and the next thing you know, he's dead." Then Tom noted the luscious Vicki Higgins talking to his brother, "Wow who is that?" He said nodding his head her way.

"That be the luscious Vicki Higgins. She is with CMI."

"Really, what does she do?"

"No one knows. But she does it fine."

"I saw your woman there, she be one good looking lady," Trevayne smiled and gave Tom a soft punch on the arm.

"I'm lucky she likes sports, that is how I met her at a ball game. Bigger football fan than baseball, 'Niner fan."

"Likes a team with a quarterback a smart move on her part. Somewhat unusual for a lawyer to figure that out, but good for her." Trevayne said. Like all Bear fans Trevayne could never understand why they could never get a quarterback.

"What are all the CMI people doing up front? Looks like they are having some kind of a meeting," he said to Trevayne.

Just then they heard the refrain of another *Our Father* being prayed. People around them would kneel or sit and some now let out a sigh. Trevayne couldn't believe it, the most paranoid praying group of people he had ever been around. He looked up to the front of the parlor like he would know who was praying but he didn't. He looked to Tom like Tom might know but Tom only gave a shrug.

The prayers seemed to go on forever. Kept repeating them over and over till the right number was reached then everyone went back to talking and carrying on.

"You Catholics sure do pray a lot."

"Paranoia does that to you, but I try to curtail it." Tom said.

"You do? Man, it seems ever since I walked through the door to this place people have been dropping to their knees to pray at the drop of a hat"

"We believe a prayer or two will get you to the Promised Land."

"More like a prayer or six," Trevayne said.

"Personally I believe it is more important to be a good person than a good Catholic."

"You succeed?"

"Well as Bill Clinton would say, 'that would depend on your definition of good'."

"So the answer be no."

"Pretty much so."

THIRTEEN

"I'm supposed to give the eulogy tomorrow," Marie said to

Sarah. She sounded somewhat dazed. They were outside the funeral

parlor in the common hallway near the ladies room

Sarah felt for her, getting up in front of people and speaking, "did you have time to prepare anything?"

"I don't have to. My dad prepared his own." She held up the envelope her mother had given her so Sarah could see it. "This is it." She said waving it.

"How did he do that? Did he know he was going to die? A premonition?" Sarah was somewhat amazed.

"No, according to my mother he wrote the first draft about four years ago, and he revised it and updated it on a regular basis ever since. It was about the time we bought them a computer so they could email us from Florida. He started writing it then, saving it, revising it. Now I get to read it. It could say anything."

"I'm sure it will cover things that he wanted said."

"That could be anything. This envelope feels pretty thick." She figured her dad wrote all kinds of strange stuff. Stuff he wanted to get off his chest. And what better way to do it then when you're dead.

Sarah looked and saw that it was a business sized envelope, thick and taped. "I kind of figured it would be Frank who would have given the eulogy."

"According to my mother he wanted me. I guess I should be flattered. I just wish I knew what this says."

"Open it and read it."

"According to Mom I can't open it till the day of the funeral to keep it fresh."

"Who is going to know?"

"She will, she knows everything."

Sarah nodded in agreement. She knew that from dealing with her own parents they just had a way of knowing things.

Just then Emily came out of the parlor and started walking towards them. "You didn't open that did you?" She asked her daughter looking at the envelope.

"No Ma."

"Well don't. It is about the only request your father ever made of anyone. Respect it." She then entered the ladies room.

Marie and Sarah watched her walk away. "I guess that takes care of that," Sarah said.

"Should make tomorrow interesting."

* * *

After leading the mourners in the prayers for the dead Father Harris had cornered Muldoon. This is the last thing Muldoon wanted to be stuck talking to this guy. In one corner of the funeral parlor he saw Frank, Bosco and Tucker talking, Bosco doing most of the talking the other two listening. Now and then Tucker would nod as if he was agreeing with what was being said. Frank looked perplexed.

In another corner he saw Harry and Marie trying to be civil to each other. Marie would talk to him without fully looking at him.

She would look at him out of the corner her eye with her head down as she spoke.

"Was in the seminary with Frank." Father Harris told Muldoon.

Larry could only nod, "yeah, Frank mentioned that."

"Didn't know your dad, but he looked like a fine man."

Looked like a fine man? What did that mean? But again Muldoon only nodded and kept looking over at Frank, Bosco and Tucker. Then he saw Bosco look around for a chair. He looked ghostly white. Bosco's face his entire head looked as if it was being drained of blood.

Muldoon left the priest and made his way over to Bosco, "you okay?"

"He just received some bad news," Tucker said.

Muldoon had no idea what they could be. "What bad news?"

"Ten grand."

"Ten grand? What does that mean?"

"The cost of getting back in the Church's good graces."

"Really, ten grand." Muldoon looked to his brother Frank.

Frank smiled, "salvation does not come cheap."

"What does he need the ten grand for?" Harris asked as he followed Muldoon over to the group.

"Heaven." Tucker said

"Wow, who gets the money?" Harris asked.

They all turned to Frank.

"Those who know what strings to pull and what wheels to grease." He told them.

"He is not one of those sex perverts the Church has been having so much trouble with lately is he?" Harris asked.

"Nah, he is not even a priest," Tucker said. "Well not one that counts."

"What do you mean by sex perverts?" Frank asked Harris. He didn't like being reminded of the Church's sex problems.

"A lot of perversion here in the states Frank," Father Harris said. He shook his head, "sad very sad. Perhaps they don't know about it in Rome."

Frank looked at Harris trying to keep his temper under control. Why does everyone think Rome is out to lunch he wondered. "Rome knows more than you think." He said somewhat emphatically.

"It's not what they know it is what they are not doing." Tucker said. "You know I think some of those Bishops and Cardinals might make some good insurance regulators. They always seem dazed and confused."

"Ten grand." It was Bosco. He was sitting. Some color returning to his features. "How can it be ten grand?" He looked to Muldoon like he may have the answer

"Why does he need ten grand?" Harris asked

"To get back in the Church's good graces." Tucker repeated. Tucker was beginning to think this guy Harris might a bit slow on the uptake.

"What makes him think he is not now?"

"He has sinned," Tucker started to explain. "He was a priest, then left to marry a floozie now getting a divorce as she *is* a floozie but no longer *his* floozie. Now he wants the marriage annulled so he can go back to being a sermonizing soul saving man of God."

"Wow," was all Harris could say. It looked like he may have to sit down.

Muldoon looked to Frank, "Ten grand?" Seemed kind of steep even to Muldoon. "You would think they would be glad to get him back especially when there is a priest shortage. You would think they would want him back. At least he is heterosexual." That was good enough reason for Larry.

Tucker said, "They are in short supply these days."

"Priests or heterosexuals?"

"Actually both."

Bosco was still sitting. He could hear them talking but didn't really know what they were saying. His mind was starting to race. *How to get ten grand?* He would have to talk to Gladkowski. Perhaps come up with a better plan. He was going to have to talk some more to Frank. Have to get him alone away from Tucker and the others. And who was this other priest that was horning in? He seemed to be a straight arrow, probably not the type of guy who should be privy to this type of conversation. He seemed like the type of guy who thought everything the Church did was on the up and up. Hell, the way they handle their sexual abuse problems is pretty good evidence the up and up is never going to be a precept of the Church.

Not like stonewalling anyway.

* * *

Muldoon almost actually felt sorry for Bosco. Here he wanted to get his life in some kind of order and would probably go broke trying. It didn't seem right.

"Don't I know you?" From out of nowhere it was Sarah's father Hal. He was pointing at Bosco. "You sure look familiar."

Bosco looked up not knowing who he was looking at. He obviously didn't know Hal. He simply had a blank stare on his face still trying to figure where to get $10,000. He thought the little scam he had going with Gladkowski would pay for his divorce lawyer, the divorce settlement and getting back in the Church's good graces. But now the Church was taking all of it. It just wasn't right.

"Doesn't he look familiar?" Hal said to his wife Joyce.

Joyce looked at Bosco. Studying him. "I think he had hair then."

"Yeah, that's it," Hal said happily. "He had hair."

Nothing was registering with Bosco.

Tucker who was watching suddenly decided to get involved. "He is somewhat bewildered. He has received some bad news."

"Oh my," said Joyce. "Nothing serious I hope."

"You were at St. Harold the Holy weren't you?" Hal accused Bosco. That is where Hal knew him. He felt triumphant. Bosco was a priest in their parish church some years ago. Hal remembered him well. He gave useless, pointless sermons, but he kept them short. Truly a gift if there ever was one.

"You remember him, don't you dear?" Hal asked

Joyce suddenly became embarrassed. She turned to her husband and walked up close to him and whispered, "I think he left the church to get married." Joyce then took a step back from Bosco as if he was diseased. Priests who leave the priesthood to get married were just not right in her opinion. Turning their back on God to fulfill the temptation of the flesh or whatever they were trying to fulfill just was not right in her book.

Muldoon simply watched and listened. He did not see Hal and Joyce walk in. He looked around and did not see Sarah. He was surprised her parents were here without her nearby. No one was nearby other than Tucker and Bosco. Frank had wandered off. Father Harris also had disappeared. Bosco looked like he wanted to wander off. What Bosco really wanted to do was to find Gladkowski and come up with a more lucrative scheme. He could not believe that after all this time he runs into a parishioner. The Church where he was assigned was located in the far south suburbs. He now lived north. Never ventured to the south side for any reason just to avoid this type of situation. He comes one time and runs into people who know him. This getting back in the Church's good graces was turning into a lot of work.

"Did you ever get married?" Hal asked. Hal could not believe a priest would leave the priesthood to get married. Didn't they know when they had it made? Get up, say a few prayers, celebrate a mass, maybe bury someone, visit some sick person and say a couple of more prayers. Get in a round of golf. Maybe during the school year you visited a classroom. Every now and then you marry someone. Get invited to the reception. No gift needed, just drop in say a prayer, have a drink or two, eat the meal and leave.

Sunday might be busy, but still if you planned it right you could still be done by noon.

Might have its lonely moments here and there, but what is wrong with a little loneliness Hal wondered. Hal had times in his life he actually liked being alone. He didn't get too many but when he got them he savored them.

"Yes he did get married," Tucker informed Hal and Joyce. Tucker spoke, as it appeared that Bosco was still off in never never land and would not get around to answering the question. "Unfortunately the woman he married did not turn out to be as faithful as one would like." Tucker sadly shook his head.

"Ah, that is too bad," Hal said in a consoling manner. "So he is kind of out of luck now, I imagine."

"Far from it" Tucker said. "The Reverend may have connections in Rome itself and may be able to get back in the Church's good graces. But of course it comes with a heavy price."

"I imagine the penance would be a bit stiff," Joyce said.

"And somewhat pricey."

"Really?" Hal said.

"Ten grand," Tucker said knowingly.

"Cheaper than a car." Hal said.

"Oh Larry," Joyce said reaching out to Muldoon. "We are ignoring you. So sorry for your loss." She then hugged him.

Then Hal reached for him shook his hand and gave him a hug as well. Muldoon was somewhat surprised by this as Hal never hugged him, and rarely shook his hand.

"Any news on Omaha?" Joyce asked with a concerned look on her face.

Muldoon answered quickly, "We simply haven't had much time to discuss it."

Hal and Joyce simply stood side by side and shook their heads knowingly, as this was the answer they were expecting.

Out of the corner of his eye Muldoon saw Bosco rise up out of the chair he had sunken into and head off in the direction of Frank. Tucker followed closely.

Then the luscious Vicki Higgins tapped him on his shoulder. He turned she too reached out and gave him a hug and simply said, "Hang in there Larry. I will see you at work."

The hug felt good. Grieving did have its upside

FOURTEEN

Slowly the mourners left until all that was left in the parlor was the Muldoon family. Before departing Father Harris once again knelt and said the prayers for the dead as did Frank.

Bosco didn't.

When it came time for him to leave he simply got up and left. His mind appeared to be elsewhere. Muldoon watched him leave and saw that he was reaching for a cell phone as he left the parlor.

Tom and Cindy were sitting together off to the right. Marie was with her children while her husband stood near the back looking lost and out of place. Frank sat next to his mother on a couch located in front of the casket. Larry and Sarah were to the left but not seated. Their kids had gone home with Nancy.

Muldoon took a look at his dad wondering where he was now. Was there a life after death? Or was that just a bunch of gibberish? His mother looked tired. She simply sat and looked towards the casket at her husband.

They had been through a lot together raising a family, making friends, having their arguments. Like most normal people they did go to bed mad as they lived in the world where differences could not be settled simply with a hug and a kiss after the ten o'clock news. There were times when it was good to let your partner have it. Not once in their forty plus years together did the word divorce ever come up. But they had their differences. A good fight here and there is a sign you still cared.

The parlor was quiet almost eerie. His mother motioned Larry over to where she was sitting. "I want the following pallbearers, Sarah, Marie, his brother Jack, Marie's oldest John and our friends from Florida Ethel and Wally."

Larry nodded.

She turned to Frank. "I want you to celebrate the mass. You do not need to give the eulogy. Your dad wrote his own. Marie will give it."

"He wrote his own eulogy?" Frank was surprised but at the same time he wasn't surprised. It sounded like something his dad would do. At one time he and some other priests wondered why more people didn't simply write their own. Save priests and ministers a lot of grief. Especially for that crowd that never went to church. They are the ones that always expect the minister to say something profound.

"What does it say?" He asked.

"You will know tomorrow."

Later back at the house Tom and was watching the ballgame. The Yankees had a big lead, 14-2 and though the game would probably go on until 2 in the morning, it did appear that Series would return to New York with the Yankees up three games to two.

Frank was having a beer trying to unwind when his mother entered the kitchen.

"He should have had a priest." She was not going to let up.

He took a long drink from the can, "I will look into it."

"What is there to look into? He should have had a priest and he didn't."

Frank saw no point in arguing. He decided it was best to get back to the rectory and put up with the inanity of Father Harris. He would also have to call St. Thomas the Doubter parish and let them know he would celebrate his father's funeral mass. He finished the beer, set the can down, and kissed his mother on the cheek, "see you in the morning, and get some rest."

Larry was out on the deck. First Tom and Cindy came out to tell him they were leaving and would meet him at the funeral parlor in the morning. Then Sarah came out to tell him she was going to bed and that Marie already had. Frank stuck his head out and told him he would see him in the morning.

His mother then came out to join him. There was a wrought iron table and four chairs. She sat in one and motioned for him to sit in another. Though going on late October the night air was unseasonably warm. His mother was wearing a sweater but it was not buttoned.

"You okay?" He asked

"Why wouldn't I be okay?"

"Just thought you might want some time alone."

"I will have plenty of time to be alone."

He had no answer he simply looked at her. She was a strong woman; her strength came from quiet. What the poets call inner strength.

She said, "You know your dad and I never talked of death. We knew we would die, and one of us would die first but we always thought there would be a warning. Health would start to fail, a stroke or heart attack. Never thought one of us would simply keel over at the drop of a hat.

"Cindy might be right; maybe we should sue that hospital. But the more I think about it I would like to sue the Church."

He was sitting across from her listening. He had the feeling he may hear something profound. A parent comes clean.

"They should be made to keep their word. I feel sorry for your dad. He probably counted on a priest. I am sure he figured he would have a chance to get the slate clean before dying. That's what they told us, over and over and over and over again.

"It's all a bunch of lies." She was disgusted, "I remember when eating meat on Friday was a sin. Then one day you woke up, *whoops, you can eat all you want, never mind.* I will tell you something else. Missing mass on Sunday is no sin. What is the other big one, oh yeah, birth control. Like people don't do that. If that is a sin, no Catholic has made it to heaven.

"What do you think of Cindy?"

Listening to his mother at times was a lot like listening to Tucker. The same tendency to jump from subject to subject. "She seems nice." He answered.

"And a lawyer. Nothing better than a smart woman." She loved smart women, mainly because they scared all men, smart and dumb. "She does seem a little sue happy but that is the lawyer in her. I am going to talk to her before I return to Florida. She might be on to something."

"So you're going to go back?" He asked He thought there might be a chance she would stay here where her roots were.

"Of course why would I stay here? Our friends are there. And you can say what you want about Florida. They know how to treat the elderly. Here they just want your vote then toss you aside, kind of like the Church."

"You are kind of stuck on this Church thing aren't you?" He said.

"We were sold a bill of goods and they did not deliver. Their taking your father and me for granted is going to cost them. I have a new lease on life. I am going to hound them to the grave. Your father's death has woke me up. I have new meaning in my life.

"You watch now that Marie and Harry are getting divorced the Church will screw them over too." Her voice was starting to rise, "and Tom getting married is some chapel in Las Vegas. They will try to tell the world that that doesn't count.

"At one time I would have cared about all that, your sister's divorce. Tom getting married in some street side chapel. But now I just want them to be happy. Of course Marie did marry somewhat of a goof. Your dad had that guy pegged from the beginning. I always thought he was nice, different but nice. That was one thing your dad could do, judge people.

"You know," she told him. "You are the only one we never worried much about. Sarah is smart. You couldn't have done much better."

He felt like he should stand up and take a bow. But then why shouldn't he get some credit for a good marriage? Why does everyone figure it is the woman? Sarah was great, but he must have some quality.

"I have no idea on what Frank does in Rome. When he first went over there we were quite proud. But now I think I would rather see him be a pastor of something back here. I think they are all nuts in Rome and I think he might be afflicted as well."

They became quiet for a while. There was very little sound. Now and then they would hear a car go by on a nearby street. A rabbit came into the yard, barely seen through the darkness. They both watched it. The rabbit acted as if they weren't even there.

"Your dad would like you to have his golf clubs. Hopefully you will be better than he was. He was terrible. I would like you Sarah and the kids to come down. I don't care if you have to come in the summer when it is 100 in the shade. I want company and some family down there on occasion. I know Marie will come and probably mope about her marriage. I am not looking forward to that. I think once Tom marries Cindy he will disappear. She will be suing every third person she sees and he will be travelling all over with that stupid baseball. Frank is married to the Church. So it leaves you. Anyway you and Sarah are more like your dad and me. So it won't be as bad as you think. And the kids will like it."

"We'll come."

"You going to Omaha?"

He had almost forgotten about that. Mothers seemed to remember everything. He hadn't given Omaha much thought. Thought more about Bosco and his plight than what he and Sarah should do.

"If the job is there I'm pretty sure I will take it and we will go."

"You might as well. Just remember you come to Florida at least once a year."

"We will."

She slowly got up and walked over to where he was sitting. She leaned over and kissed his cheek. "Don't worry I will be okay." He watched her walk in to the house and wondered if he would be okay.

FIFTEEN

Bosco was sitting in his car waiting for Gladkowski. It was 7AM. The fall chill was in the air. He was hoping Gladkowski would come in early. He left a message on Gladkowski's voice mail that they had to talk. He had no way of knowing whether Gladkowski had received it. When Bosco got home last night all he did was pace his apartment for a good two hours trying to figure out a way to get more money. Never in his life did he think getting a marriage annulled and back in the Church's good graces would cost $10,000. He thought $5,000 was out of line, but now $10,000. Hopefully it would be tax deductible.

He looked at his watch. Where was he? He wanted to get to the funeral and get a chance to talk to Muldoon's brother one more time before he returned to Rome. Maybe he could get the price reduced.

Then last night Sheila called. Right out of the blue. She wanted some CDs that she said she bought and are rightfully hers. What a petty bitch. He was going to tell her no but then he thought he best cooperate because once she hears about the annulment the petty bitch will become a stark raving maniac.

A car pulled into the lot and parked next to him. At last, it was Gladkowski.

"Good morning John. What brings you here so bright and early on a nice Friday morning?"

"Didn't you get my message?" Bosco said getting out of the car with a look of concern.

"Nope, what's up?"

"The price."

"What price?"

"The price for the annulment."

They started walking towards the office with Gladkowski rummaging through his pants pocket for the key. "I thought you had a pipeline to god through some priest somewhere."

"So did I," Bosco said following Gladkowski into the office. "Turns out the pipe line is an expensive one."

"Well we're doing okay." Gladkowski said. "Only been at it less than a week and wee got some money coming in. Though I think that Jew may be a problem."

"How was the woman I sent?" Bosco wanted to know.

"She was kind of good looking I almost hated jerking her around. But then when it is for god, why not?" He smiled at Bosco. "I'm going to make some coffee if you want to wait a minute."

Bosco sat and watched Gladkowski go through the motions of making the coffee. The coffepot was the only clean thing in the office. Gladkowski had to go in the bathroom for the water but in no time he had everything set up and working.

"So what's the problem?" He asked Bosco.

"The price is ten grand."

"Holy shit. You ever think of becoming a Lutheran?

"Too many Synods."

All Gladkowski could do was shake his head, "really. Is that a bad thing, too many Synods?"

Gladkowski did not know what a Synod was and didn't care if he ever did. He figured if it had anything to do with religion it was probably fucked up.

"They are always bickering. At least we Catholics believe in the same thing on paper"

Gladkowski walked over to the coffeepot and poured himself a cup and motioned for Bosco to do the same, as Gladkowski wasn't going to wait on the nut.

"We just got to move it along quicker, going to need more cars, at least sixty."

"Jesus H. Christ.'

"Please don't swear."

"We are going as fast as we can." Gladkowski was all for making a few extra bucks but you had to keep things, at least appearance wise, on the up and up.

"My window of opportunity is only so wide." Bosco started to explain. "My connection goes back to Rome soon. I will try to get him to come down in his price but according to him there are a lot of palms to grease. And $10,000 is the low figure. And on top of that I may have to make a 60 day retreat."

"What for?"

"To pray."

"That's a lot of praying."

"I need a lot of help."

Gladkowski thought ever since he came across Bosco and his annulment plan that starting a religion may not be a bad business to get into. A lot of goofs like Bosco about. If you kept it simple and cheap you could make it. Could start out with a little storefront. No sermons, no hymns, no wailing and weeping. No raffle drives. The last time Gladkowski was in Church he was not only supposed to sell raffle tickets but buy them as well, and then buy an ad in the Church bulletin and volunteer for the parish festival. Actually saying a prayer did not seem to be part of the agenda.

He thought by starting a religion he could eliminate all that bullshit because there had to be a lot of people like him out there that just wanted to go to church and be left alone. Not to mention the goofs like Bosco roaming the countryside looking for god.

If you could get 400 members at $25.00 a week, you would pull in ten grand a week. Have three sets of services on Sunday, 7:30 – 8:30, 9:00 – 10:00 and 10:30 to 11:30. Be done by noon. About a five hour work week. What could be better? People could come in with their prayer books, shawls, whatever and simply sit or kneel for one hour and pray in their own way. No sermon to listen to, no hymns to try and sing. No raffles, no festivals, no bingo just sit and pray or stare or whatever you wanted to do. Call it *The Time for God and God Alone Church.* Scatter some religious pictures about the place. Ten percent of the weekly revenue could go to charity, pay the rent and pocket the rest. Praise the Lord.

Get tax-free status. Just bribe some political flunky and you could get that. He was surprised someone didn't try it. Some blacks have their storefronts, but they weep and wail and shout Amen every ten seconds or so. Very nerve racking. Gladkowski wanted peace and quiet. Just had to find some religious sort to get it up and running.

Bosco would be a good guy for it. Devout or what passes for devout. Sincere and just dumb enough.

Gladkowski looked up from his coffee. Bosco was sitting across from him with a thoughtful look, "Have you ever thought of starting your own church?"

* * *

Tucker arrived at the office early. He wanted to check his email, hoping he had none. And he hoped he would get Trevayne to drive to the funeral, as Tucker didn't want to drive through Boogie Land to get to the church. Trevayne had not yet arrived. Wanda the dip in charge of clerical had yet to show up, so there would be no coffee, so he brought a cup with him that he bought in the lobby of the building. It was a little after seven when he arrived and he was the only one there. So much for starting early and staying late he thought to himself. He fired up his computer and sipped his coffee waiting for the screen to come up, and sure enough he had an email. Actually he had 25.

He looked and most were garbage, but there was one from Schwartz. He opened it and saw that Schwartz sent it at 9PM California time, which was damn near midnight Chicago time. What a jerk thought Tucker, didn't know enough to go home. It is one thing to start early and stay late if you are on the way up, but when you get to up you should have enough sense to go home on a week night. He would have to mention to his wife what an idiot CMI had in Home Office, not knowing enough to call a day a day. It would make good dinner conversation. Let her know that work wasn't all that it was cracked up to be. He opened it and it turned out to be useless drivel. A complete waste of time. Just verifying that he would be here Monday, looking forward to seeing everyone. God how awful it must be to think you are important. All Tucker could think was what a waste of time sending that. Not to mention that Tucker had to read it. He could waste time without reading useless email.

"You going to the funeral?" He looked up it was Doris Simpson.

"Yes." He should have known she would be in.

"I would like to go too. Do you mind if I ride with you?"

"No, you can come along. I was hoping to get Trevayne to drive, but I'm sure he has enough room." He didn't remember seeing her at the wake, but perhaps she was there when he wasn't. What the hell was he going to talk to her about in the car on the way out there? He probably should have asked if she had work to do but thought better of it. Doris always got her job done. Missing a few hours would not change that.

"What time do you think you will leave?"

The funeral mass was scheduled for 10 and Tucker told her they would leave by nine, no later. "Maybe even a quarter to."

No sooner had Doris left than Trevayne Robinson was in his doorway. "The luscious Vicki would like to go to the funeral and I said she could ride with me."

Tucker looked up, "I was hoping you would drive."

"And leave you alone in the back seat with the luscious Vicki."

Sex crazed smokes could drive you nuts. "I doubt if she wants anything to do with me and anyway Doris wants to come along."

"That should keep things on the straight and narrow." Robinson said shaking his head from side to side. "Doris can sit in the back with you." Robinson was pleased with this solution.

"We thought you could drive since you are from that part of town."

"Afraid you may make a wrong turn and end up is some neighborhood where the brothers will do you in?"

"More or less." No use lying to him.

"You are lucky I drove down this morning."

"Just a hunch. I thought with you now in retirement mode you would be willing to take time off to go to the funeral."

"No one has to die for me to coast." Then he added, "I didn't plan on coming back after the funeral. I was going to pretty much call it a day as I usually take the train in. But then yesterday when the luscious Vicki batted those baby blues, what could I say. And she really looks hot in her widow weeds by the way, I changed my plans."

"She's not a widow."

"Whatever, she looks good in black."

"Have you seen the Reverend?" Tucker asked him

Trevayne walked in to the office and sat and looked at Tucker and asked, "just what is the deal with you white people and religion? You people drop to your knees at the drop of the hat. I thought we were bad with all our yelling and what not but you people are nuts."

"Well it is not easy being good. Basically no one is good, that is why we pray for the dead." Tucker took a sip from the coffee, "actually none of us do much good on earth which is why we continue to pray for the dead. To be honest I don't know if it does any good for the dead, but it does some good for the living."

"Assuming they can kneel at the drop of a hat."

"Look at the bright side. We are not going to the funeral parlor before, just the church. There will be praying at the parlor this morning before they leave."

"No way could I get through that."

Then Vicki knocked on the door and stepped in. "The Reverend called, he won't be in this morning, he is going right to the funeral. He says he must see Larry's brother before he leaves for Rome. Then he wanted to know if I would ever worked in a church."

"You mean like a nun?" Trevayne said.

"I could never be a nun."

Trevayne let out a sigh.

It was then Tucker saw Vicki. She was standing behind Robinson and while talking took a step to her left and came into full view. She was in black, but not a dreadful black, it was a black that said I am sad for a friend, but I still screw. "You look very nice Vicki," Tucker blurted out. He wanted to sit in the back with her now. Not that anything would happen, but just to be seen with her would make it a grand day.

"Why thank you," it was the first time she could ever remember Tucker paying her a compliment for any reason. She smiled turned to leave and said, "Let me know when you are ready to leave."

Right after we lose our hard ons.

SIXTEEN

Muldoon pulled into the parking lot and saw that Tom and Cindy had already arrived as had Frank. He helped his mother from the car. The morning was cool. The wind was coming off the lake and the fall leaves were blowing around the parking lot. As they were making their way to the door of the parlor Marie and Sarah pulled in with the kids in the back. All the family was there except for Harry and his and Marie's kids.

It was just eight thirty as they entered the parlor. The family was quiet and all eyes were on Emily as if watching her would make it easier for everyone. They all said a prayer at the casket and then either stood or sat near the front of the parlor.

Larry was standing next to Frank when Bosco entered the parlor. He looked around, walked to the kneeler, said a prayer and then walked over to Frank and Larry.

"We got to talk." He blurted out.

"This is not the place," Larry said.

Bosco ignored him, as he was not going to give up. "That price cannot be right. The Church has been selling annulments forever and it has never been that high." Bosco had known that any one who wanted an annulment could get one, just had to pay, but never ten grand and jump through a few hoops like a circus act.

"You have broken the mold." Frank said.

"I don't want to break any mold. I want to use the old mold."

"Your situation is very unique," Frank explained. "You are the first of a kind. You are a precedent."

Emily got up and walked over and said to Bosco, "I want to thank you for your prayers last night. That was very thoughtful."

Bosco wondered why this woman couldn't just leave him alone. Always popping up and thanking him.

She added, "If there is anything I can do for you let me know."

Both Frank and Larry looked to their mother wondering where did that come from? Sounded like she might be a fixer.

Larry said, "Well he needs cash."

"A tough commodity for some to come by," Frank added.

"What for?" She asked.

"To get back in the Church's good graces," Larry said.

"Is that possible?" She asked

"For a price," Bosco said.

"What did you do to fall out of their graces?" Emily asked.

Larry told her. Told her about Bosco being a priest, then a lover. Leaving the priesthood for a job in insurance. Becoming a married man. Then a separated man, then a divorced man. Now striving to become an annulled man, so he can once again become a priest and back in the church's good graces.

"You left the church to go into insurance?" She looked to each of her sons, shook her head and walked away.

"That does sound stupid," Frank said.

"How much do you need before you head back to Rome?" Bosco asked. He had to get the ball rolling. He thought once he got it rolling maybe the momentum of the thing would see him through."

"Half."

Larry was somewhat surprised at how calmly and efficiently his brother said that. What did he do in Rome? Maybe he did this kind of thing all the time. Buying and selling annulments and whatever other sins you could buy your way out of but the again going for an annulment couldn't be a sin that is just a money making opportunity.

"Five thousand dollars! Good god almighty!" Bosco then walked over to a chair and sat shaking his head from side to side. Having a religious vocation can certainly be a pain in the ass.

Other mourners were starting to drift into the parlor. They would each walk to the front to say a prayer and offer words of comfort to Emily and her family and take a seat. Harry arrived with his and Marie's kids. As soon as she saw him she walked briskly over to him and the kids. Said something to him and then escorted their kids to the front of the parlor. He stood alone for a few minutes before making his way to the front.

"You should tell your sister to calm down," Harry said to Larry.

"Well she has a new friend and that new friend is a lawyer.' Larry said.

"Ah shit." He then walked over to the side of the parlor where very few people were and took a seat by himself.

Cindy walked over to Larry, "what did he want?"

"Peace."

"He should have thought of that before he unzipped his zipper."

All Larry could do was shrug. He kind of felt sorry for Harry now for some reason. He thought maybe they could work it out. But the more he watched Marie he knew she was in no mood to work anything out. Her body language said *I am going to get that bastard and I am going to get him good.*

Slowly the parlor was full of mourners. They were all talking. Some were there because it meant a morning off from work others because of their fondness for the family and the deceased.

Mr. Ford announced that Frank was going to lead them in the prayers for the dead. When they were completed the mourners would make one pass past the casket then make their way to their cars for the procession to the church. The family would remain till all were outside.

It dawned on Larry this would be the last time he would see his dad. He felt tears starting to swell up inside. His mother was clutching a handkerchief. Marie was next to her doing the same.

After the mourners were outside the Muldoon family made their final pass. Larry took his mother's arm and led her past the casket. They stopped briefly blessed themselves and made they way to their cars.

The procession to the church was uneventful. Emily was pleased with the number of people who had shown up at the parlor and who joined the funeral procession. "Your dad would have liked that," she said to Larry.

Frank had gone ahead and now met the casket at the church, blessed it and said some prayers. Larry noted Trevayne, the only black man in the church, Tucker, Doris and Vicki off to one side near the back. That is nice of them he thought.

SEVENTEEN

Marie made her way up to the altar clutching the envelope her mother had given her. Frank had announced to the congregation that his dad had written his own eulogy and asked that Marie give it. This caused a murmur to run through the church, as this was the first time any of them would hear a eulogy written by the deceased. Many sat up straighter in their pews as if that would help them hear it better.

Tucker who was starting to daydream suddenly became alert. Trevayne thought that this could be interesting a white man reaching out from the grave. Trevayne looked and saw Bosco on the other side of the church. Bosco appeared to be in deep thought and not aware that he was about to hear a eulogy written by a dead man.

Marie reached the small podium, adjusted the microphone and took the eulogy out of the envelope and looked out at the congregation. She thought she would be nervous but she wasn't. She felt very calm. She didn't know why other than if people didn't like it they couldn't blame her.

She didn't write it.

She read it earlier that morning so she wouldn't be in for any surprises when she read it in public. She kept this from her mother as she felt if she was going to give it any justification she should be prepared. It read exactly like something her dad would have said, and she wanted to deliver it right.

She made a brief announcement. "As my brother has told you, my dad has written his own eulogy. I will read it for you, as I think he would have wanted." She then ran her hand along the paper as it set on the podium to take the creases out and began.

"I don't know if I can see any of you right now or not. I hope I can because I would like to see your faces as you hear this. I have asked my daughter to read it as I have heard my son Frank stand before you and preach many a time. And Marie is my only daughter, and though I have never tried to play favorites with my children she is my favorite. I guess all parents have a favorite, we just can't admit it while we are alive.

"Love. That is what I want to tell you about first. I was watching Oprah one afternoon and everyone was telling each other how much they loved each other. The host loved the guests. The guests loved the host. They loved everyone in the audience. The audience loved them.

"It was such a love fest I thought I was going to get sick and die right there.

"Emily and I have been married for over 40 years, actually closer to 50 than 40. Naturally we have loved each other, as matter of fact very much. But what the idiots on TV over look is just as

important. They over look like. You have to like someone to make it work. I can say without hesitation that I love everyone in this Church this morning. But basically I only like about 6 of you.

"So when people asked me how Emily and I stayed married I would simply tell them that I liked her. I liked doing things with her. Not necessarily every waking minute, but I liked very much our time together. Love is the cheapest commodity we now have. The la de dah set has gotten a hold of it and pretty much has ruined it. Nothing wrong with it, great to love people. But if you want marriages or friendships to last you better like people as well. You might want to try liking them first.

"Emily was not only my wife, she was my best friend. She blessed us with four wonderful children. I was always hoping she would go first so she wouldn't have to be alone. But then again perhaps she can use the quiet. She never said she loved quiet but I know she liked it."

Marie hesitated and looked out over the congregation. She had their rapt attention. Especially when she read that her father only liked about six people present. That caused everyone to look around and wonder.

"Why? Some of you may be asking yourselves what possessed me to write my own eulogy. Well no one knows me better than me. There are certain things I want said. I didn't want you all to sit there and listen to the usual. 'He was a good man. He was a loving father, a loving husband.' Everybody gets that one. Even the slugs of the world get that. I want to tell you some of the things I learned during my life and the observations I have made.

As you all know I was raised a Catholic, grammar school, high school. Mass on Sunday, Holy days and a few in between. Altar boy. Was here for the Latin Rite and now the English. Knew what it meant not to eat meat on Friday, fast and abstain during Lent. Fast before Holy Communion. One thing I have learned through all of it is something that should be engraved in every church cornerstone in the world. And that is simply this. Any sermon longer than seven minutes is a complete waste.

326

This brought a smile and some laughter to those in attendance a couple even applauded. Many agreed but most knew nothing would come of it.

Marie continued, *"Over the years I have wondered about many things in life. Things that I have questioned, but no one else, unfortunately has. For example, exactly what was Neil Young thinking when he joined up with Crosby Stills and Nash? Was he temporarily insane?*

"Has anyone heard a traffic report on the radio and actually changed their route to or from work? If they have, which I doubt, why is the traffic backed up at the same spots each and every rush hour?

"Why aren't situation comedies funny?

"Why do some restaurants feel it is necessary to sing "Happy Birthday" to you on your birthday? It is simply a horrible experience.

"Why do TV Evangelists and loud mouth Reverends get to ignore the adultery and not bearing false witness commandments?

The rest of us don't get this break. Why can't we all pick and choose?

"Why are TV Meteorologist free of all responsibility for their incorrect weather forecasts? All they have to say is 'today's weather will be like yesterdays', and they will be right 80% of the time A percentage for correctness they have never achieved.

"If integration and diversity are so important, which they are not, why do the Chinese get to live in segregated China Towns?

"As you know in my younger days I was a musician. Played in a band, bass guitar. Was there for Elvis and The Beatles. Though I am a dozen years or so older than most of the groups from the British invasion, I loved their music. Thank god for Elvis or we would still be humming 'How Much Is That Doggie in the Window'

"But will some one please tell me why everyone who has walked past a recording studio between 1944 and 1998 is in the Rock and Roll Hall of Fame.

"Is that the only requirement?

"We have lived in Florida almost full time for the past dozen years. For the record Florida is a screwed up state. But so is here. Yet in Florida they seem to be able to do it for less money. Did all the cheap crooked politicians move south?

"When I was a young man, like most young men I had my dreams. Was going to find the cure for cancer. Write the great American novel. Be a great actor. Be an All American football player, major league baseball player, bring world peace. I did not accomplish any of those things.

"I would have loved to have been a major league baseball player but I was never that greedy. Would have loved to play football, but my IQ has three digits. Might have been a doctor but my handwriting is legible. Could have written the great American novel, but Oprah scares me.

"World peace. God screwed up there. Too many religions bickering.

"What I did try to accomplish were the hard things, being a good husband, a good father, a good person and a good friend.

329

That's all. Nothing more, nothing less. And the good news is I think I pulled it off. Oh, I know I have made some enemies, but the hell with them.

"I had plenty of help from Emily, my kids, neighbors, and friends. In a way even the horrible company I worked for made me a better man and of course my God helped. Since we are in a church, at least I hope we are. Prayer is important. All the other mumble jumble isn't.

"I have loved sports but am proud to say I have never watched a complete episode of "Sports Center". In my entire life I have seen perhaps a total of 23 minutes of it. "Baseball Tonight" I rarely watched. I know this is not important. But there is not a person on TV who is smarter than the dumbest person watching him. Yet they think they are. It is very sad.

"I was, like many of you, born and raised on the south side of Chicago, and have to admit that my life has been good. There has been a reason for this that I now will share with you. It will improve

your life immeasurably. You will be happier, more successful, more content and at peace with the world.

"Each morning I would awake. Sit on the edge of my bed look to the heavens and simply say 'The Cubs suck'. No truer statement can a man utter, and my day would immediately be off to a good start. Three simple words lets say them together."

Here Marie looked out at the mourners. Lifted her right hand as if leading a choir and said, *"Repeat after me. The Cubs Suck."*

The congregation, "The Cubs suck."

"Louder."

"The Cubs Suck."

"One more time so they can hear you at Wrigley."

"The Cubs Suck." The echo through the church was breath taking.

"Now don't you all feel better? You see it is the little things that can make life easier and better.

Marie paused momentarily and saw several smiles and contented people. Maybe it does work she thought. Then she saw her estranged husband Harry and thought now there is a guy that sucks.

"I want to thank all of you who have said a prayer for the repose of my poor soul, and for offering comfort to my wife and family.

"I have one other request. When the time presents itself, have a drink in my memory, or two or three for that matter. And remember it is not who you love it is who you like."

Marie then folded the paper and walked slowly to her pew.

The congregation then turned their eyes to Frank. Frank was poised to say something, but then was afraid he might go over the allotted seven minutes. There was not much he could add. He knew his mother was right. His dad should have had a priest.

Emily listened and knew that her husband, the nice guy that he was, should have had a priest. She knew they would pay for their broken promise.

Tom and Cindy had listened. Tom had already known that the Cubs sucked. He was looking forward to suing the hospital that killed his father.

Trevayne, though not a religious man, thought this writing your own eulogy was a cool thing. Why hadn't a black thought of it? If this idea should take off there must be a way we can take credit for it If not we can always say it is racist.

Tucker thought of going home and writing his. Keeping sermons to seven minutes or less would truly be a blessing.

Doris wondered what "Sports Center" was. Couldn't be much if only watched 23 minutes in a lifetime.

Vicki didn't listen. She looked at the statues and what the other ladies in the congregation were wearing.

Larry and Sarah sat with Emily and listened. Sarah liked the idea of writing your own eulogy. She didn't know what she would say about her life. When Larry entered the church he saw Harry Schmidt seated near the back and wondered about the job with his agency, and Omaha. Two things he hadn't thought much about. He also hadn't known anyone who changed their route to and from work due to traffic reports. His dad got that right.

Bosco was off in a right rear pew by himself thinking. He never liked Crosby Stills and Nash. He was thinking about his future. This Gladkowski may have a very good idea about starting their own church. It did seem like a money making proposition

This Catholic rulebook was starting to get to him. Why should he have to get an annulment? Why the hell couldn't they simply recognize divorce? Hell, shit happens. Now he had to come with ten grand for an annulment? The more he thought about it the more he wondered about it. Why should the Church care about how he got married? He simply wanted out. If he and Shelia stayed together they would kill each other, which also is a sin. The Church would drive him nuts.

A bunch of uppity snobs is all they are.

He remembered back to when he was a priest and a couple came in wanting to get married only trouble was the guy was a Catholic and the girl wasn't. He had to tell them they would have to jump through hoops as the Church frowned on what they called *mixed marriages*. Then he told them she would have to promise to raise any kids they had as Catholics even if they were to grow up to pillage the countryside it was important that they be raised Catholic.

334

Then there was the birth control issue he tried to explain to them. The most lame teaching in the history of the Church. The sin should be *not using* birth control. That news will probably be broken to everyone on Judgment Day.

The Maker will be up there on His Throne and announce, "All who have used birth control devices please form a line on the right." Then about a kazillion people would get in the line. Then the second announcement, "All who haven't please form a line on the left." And eighteen paranoid Catholics would get in that line. And The Maker would look at the eighteen and shake his head and ask, "How could you be so dumb?"

This getting back in the Church's good graces was becoming a pain in the ass. Had to scam accident victims to raise money to pay off the Church bureaucracy when the fact was he could celebrate Mass any time he wanted. He was a priest. He simply didn't have a Church.

He knew Gladkowski was onto something. Simply a place where people can go and pray on Sunday morning. People would pay for that. People would pay to pray and be left alone. People liked being left alone.

Bosco thought the Church had too many problems they were ignoring, priests and sexual abuse, shortage of priests and the Church's fear of women. Did he really want to put himself in that mix?

Bosco looked around everyone was listening to Marie. No one had ever listened to him like that when he gave a sermon. Then he heard the loud refrain, "The Cubs Suck". He wasn't exactly sure what that was about but it sure made people happy. He would have to mention that to Gladkowski. Might be a good way to either begin or end the service.

EIGHTEEN

Outside the church the day was like a black and white movie. The sky was low and gray. It was one of those skies that looked like it would stay gray forever. The grass was dull green on the way to winter brown. The trees had shed their leaves. The fall chill was damp, a perfect day for a funeral. Everyone had filed outside the church and now were standing waiting for the casket to be placed in the hearse for the trip to the cemetery.

The cemetery wasn't that far, west on 111th to Holy Sepulcher and then a short drive to the gravesite. Fifteen to twenty minutes at most. It was decided to hold the cemetery service at the gravesite instead of inside the cemetery chapel. This was a decision made by Marie as she thought going back to the gravesite would please her father.

They were all gathered around the grave and Frank said the final prayers and then the service was over. The casket would be lowered in the ground by cemetery workers. Frank then announced that the family would be having a luncheon at Flaherty's which was located just east of the cemetery on 111th and that all were invited to join the family there.

People then started walking slowly to their cars and talking among themselves. Some who had other loved ones buried in the cemetery decided to visit their graves.

"Let's go eat," Trevayne said. "Being an Irish crowd they will probably have some liquor and with this weather I could use something to warm me up."

"No, we should just get back and let the family have their final moments." Tucker said.

Doris and Vicki sided with Tucker. Trevayne was somewhat disappointed but then he remembered he wasn't going to do any work anyway so what difference would it make.

They started walking to the car. "Anyway I should prepare myself for the coming of Schwartz this Monday." Tucker told them. He didn't really know what he had to prepare but sometimes when you sounded like you knew what you were doing people would actually start believing you did.

"What do you have to do?" Doris asked.

Tucker hesitated, as he didn't have a clue. "I should do something but I don't know what." Then to bait Robinson he said, "Maybe I can have him give Trevayne here his exit interview."

"No, no," Trevayne said instantly. "I don't want no flunky home office type giving me any exit interview. I want you."

"You want a flunky branch office type," Vicki said letting out a laugh.

"Very funny young lady," Tucker said. He could not get upset with Vicki, as she was just too cute.

They reached the car and the two men got in the front and the two women in the back. Robinson drove, not the seating arrangement he was hoping for, but sometimes fantasies turn out to be just that, fantasies.

Vicki, whose spirits seemed to be improving the further they got from the grave site and the funeral asked, "This cemetery integrated Trevayne?"

"No, we have our own. Whites need not apply."

"How do you apply?" Tucker asked.

"Dying helps."

Doris said nothing. She listened, looked out the window and would smile when someone said something she found amusing, but mainly went about her business of being Doris.

340

* * *

At the restaurant the crowd was starting to arrive. Emily was already seated at a table talking with her friends from Florida. Others were coming in and taking a seat. Two waitresses were taking drink orders.

Larry felt a tap on his shoulder and turned. Harry Schmidt was standing there, "You got a minute Larry."

"Sure."

Just then a waitress came by and took their drink orders.

"I know this is not the time or place for this but I did not want to wait till Monday as I heard Schwartz was going to be in town and I wanted you to be prepared."

"Prepared for what?"

"My offer to join the agency is off the table."

There was an awkward five seconds of silence. "To tell you the truth Harry I haven't had much time to think about it. What happened?" That was quick he thought to himself. One minute I was making a hundred grand a year, the next zilch.

"My oldest daughter Stacey's husband has lost his job. He sold computer software and now would like to become part of the agency. My wife would like that as they are expecting a child and do need some income. So to make a long story short I am taking him on."

The waitress returned with two Manhattans.

"The son you never had, "Larry said.

Schmidt took a gulp from his drink "I'm sorry. I didn't think this would happen but these companies today let people go at the drop of hat." Another gulp and the drink was gone.

"I'm sorry about your dad Larry." He shook Larry's hand. "I got to run. Talk to you soon." And he turned and left.

Muldoon watched him walk away. It only took about ten seconds but Muldoon felt that his life had just changed forever. Muldoon stood there holding his drink. He looked around the room and saw Sarah and the kids at one table with Sarah's parents. Muldoon didn't want to go there. He saw Bosco off talking to Frank again. He didn't want to go there. Marie was busy talking with Cindy. He didn't want to go there.

"I came to say goodbye Larry." It was Marie's husband.

"Have a drink and something to eat." Larry suggested.

"No I think it is best I go."

Muldoon could tell by his manner that he wanted to be far away and the sooner the better. Muldoon had nothing more to say to him. They shook hands and awkwardly wished each other well. Muldoon then watched him walk away and thought he probably wants to get back to Ohio and get laid by the Internet babe.

* * *

It was after three when Bosco got back to the office. He tried to get Frank to lower the annulment price but no go. Frank was adamant. Bosco didn't care. He knew he could get the money. He just didn't know if he wanted to pay for something he felt the church should be recognizing all along. Annulment was nothing but the Catholic word for divorce. Of course it had to be on their terms at their prices under circumstances only they would approve.

He also wanted to talk to Trevayne, as he was pretty straight shooter once you got passed the black/white gibberish. He wanted to talk to Trevayne about the new church he was thinking of starting. He found Robinson in his cubicle playing free cell on his computer.

"Hi Trevayne, you got a minute?"

"I gots all the time in the world just won fourteen games in a row. My personal best is twenty one," he said pointing to the screen. "I think I might be on a roll but I can give you a minute."

"You're not a religions man are you Trevayne," more of a statement than a question.

A worried look crossed Trevayne's features, "you all not going to try to convert me are you?" Trevayne simply felt he couldn't do all that praying Catholics seem to be able to do at the drop of a hat. But he did like the idea of the seven-minute sermon. But Bosco he found to be weird. He was a priest, then not a priest, then married, then not married now wants to be a priest again and seems to be able to pray at a moments notice.

"You think that seven minute sermon will ever come about?" Trevayne asked. He did like that idea. He thought it might be the thing to get him back to going.

"What seven minute sermon?" The first Bosco heard of it.

"During the eulogy Muldoon's dad thought no sermon should last longer than seven minutes. Weren't you listening?"

"No." Then he quickly added, "I was doing a lot of thinking then, which is why I am here."

Trevayne frowned. This was going to take a lot longer than he thought. A white guy thinking was always a bad sign. So much for the free cell record. His momentum was going to be halted by this goofy religious nut.

"I was thinking of opening a church."

"Good for you."

"I think you might like it. It is for people like you who might be attracted to it."

"Black people?"

"No, people who don't identify with a religion."

Robinson was in a chair that had coasters and he rolled it away from his desk so he could cross his legs and settle in as Bosco was not going to go away till he had gotten this off his chest. Robinson felt he should get as comfortable as possible. He then let out a sigh, "What's the deal?"

"A church for praying only. No sermons, no singing, no raffles, no festivals. None of the goofy crap you have to put up with in organized religion. You just come in and sit or kneel and pray whatever prayer you want to."

"I can do that at the library."

"You go to the library to pray?" Bosco found that odd.

"No. I am just having fun with my white brother." Robinson let out a laugh.

Bosco was disappointed. He picked Robinson to approach as he knew Robinson wasn't a big time churchgoer like Catholics are or were. He felt if he could find interest in the common man he and Gladkowski could really have this thing take off.

"I see you are back Reverend." It was Tucker

"Yeah I stayed for lunch and visited some with the Muldoon family." Bosco said.

"How is Frank?" Tucker asked.

"High with his pricing policy."

Robinson went back to free cell. He wanted that record.

Then Bosco had another brainstorm, though none of his brainstorms had yet worked. "Can I talk to you in private?" He asked Tucker.

This surprised Tucker and it showed. No one ever asked to meet with him in private unless that person was going to quit. Don't tell me this guy is going to quit? More interviews. Good god almighty what the hell is the world coming to? But then he knew Bosco would be quitting once he got back in the church's good graces. So what could he want? "Sure," he said somewhat hesitatingly.

"Let's go to your office." Bosco popped up and headed for Tuckers office in the corner.

Robinson looked up at Tucker and shrugged.

"You can put that eight on than nine and free up that column." Tucker said while studying the screen.

"Thanks."

"Great game free cell," Tucker said. "Not everyone gets paid to play it though."

"Not everyone has a chance for a new record."

Tucker took a detour past Vicki's cubicle before returning to his office to meet with Bosco. She was not there which disappointed Tucker, but the smell of her perfume was in the air. The smell of her perfume was not as good as an actual sighting but it was going to have to do.

When he arrived at his office Bosco was already seated in a chair facing Tucker's desk. Tucker walked around him and took his seat facing Bosco.

"So what can I do for you John?"

Bosco almost didn't answer as he could never recall Tucker calling him by his first name and thought he was talking to someone else. He started to look around when it dawned on him that his name was John and it was he Tucker was addressing. "I need someone to talk to." He said.

"And you picked me?" Tucker found this surprising. His wife now and then would seek out his advice but then she did what she was going to do anyway. He often wondered why she even bothered.

Bosco said, "I know you're a Catholic so maybe you can help me in my dilemma."

"You want spiritual advice from me?" Tucker found this even more surprising. He liked to think that he was a religious man, but he wasn't. He tried to go to mass each Sunday, but didn't. He use to feel guilty about it, but no longer did. He use to feel guilty as it was drilled into him forever that if he missed mass on Sunday he was doomed for all eternity. Now he figured he made it most Sundays. If church was like baseball he would be hitting about .675, pretty damn good actually.

"I was thinking of opening my own church." Bosco blurted out.

The office became silent. This was the last thing Tucker expected to hear. "What kind of church?" He finally asked.

"That is the best part," Bosco said building enthusiasm. "A church for praying only."

"Don't we have those now?"

"No."

"We don't?"

"No. Now you go and everything is orchestrated. What hymns you're going to sing what prayers you're going to say. Holding hands with the person next to you. "

During mass the congregation held hands during the *Lord's Prayer*. At first Tucker thought it was stupid, and for the most part still did, but then if you got a good looking babe next to you holding hands wasn't so bad. Course sometimes you would get stuck next to some big fat sweaty person with clammy hands. But if you planned ahead you might get lucky hand holding wise. Get there a little early, scope out the area and then settle on a pew with a good-looking babe. When he and his wife attended together it was a little trickier because a true gentleman would let his wife enter the pew first and then you are left to the element of chance. You never know who would sit next to you.

"Actually that holding hands part is somewhat goofy," Tucker didn't want to admit that on occasion he did like it.

"Some Bishop somewhere over thought that deal." Tucker continued. "That is what Bishop's do, over think a lot, except for sex abuse, where they don't think at all. So what do you do in this church beside pray."

"That's it. That is all you do. Pray."

"Just pray." Tucker thought that sounded pretty simple. "Out loud?" Tucker didn't want to pray out loud. He heard about those people that chanted and who thought they spoke in tongues. He didn't want to get involved with that crowd. They really sounded weird.

"No. Why would you want to pray out loud?"

"I have no idea." Tucker said hoping that would be the right answer.

"You simply pray in your own way. If you want to say a rosary that is what you do. If you want to think and meditate, that is what you do."

"Meditation is big," Tucker said. "I never tried it as my attention span is rather short, unless I can meditate on sex of course." Tucker said with a smile.

Bosco didn't smile. He was too excited about this idea. "It would be open to all faiths, even atheists."

"Is atheism a faith? I never knew that."

"They don't think it is, but it is."

"Wow, you learn something every day. And you would be the preacher?" Tucker asked

"No sermons."

"No sermons?" Tucker just heard a eulogy where it was suggested that all sermons should not last longer than seven minutes and now he is with a guy who wants to eliminate them all together.

Praise the Lord. "That is a great idea." Tucker now was starting to get enthused. "Where is this church?"

"Only in the discussion stage. Want to see if people are interested?"

"Wait a minute," Tucker said, "what about this annulment and getting back in the church's good graces and all that?" Just be Tucker's luck to join up and then the head guy bolts for supposed greener pastures.

"You know what they say, 'once a priest always a priest'." Bosco said.

"My mother use to tell me that. I never knew why but she did. So you are going to drop the annulment ploy."

"Well the price is kind of high. Not to mention the retreat." Bosco told him.

"Money and prayer. Doesn't sound fair. How long of a retreat?"

"Sixty days."

"Holy shit, sixty days. Maybe if you gave them a couple of thousand more they could wave that?" Tucker figured money could buy anything.

"I'm not giving them any more money. I may still go for the annulment but if this church idea works I might not even take that route. I could still say mass and all."

"Where is the church going to be?"

"Don't know. Will have to find a location."

"How do you get your money?"

"Subscriptions." This is an idea Bosco came up with while Marie was reading the eulogy.

"What do you mean subscriptions? Like a magazine?"

"Very simple. How much do you give a week now?"

"You mean when I go? Fifty bucks."

"So that would be almost $2600 a year, and what do you get for that? The same old sermons, same old prayers, same old hymns, same old raffles same old crap week in and week out."

"And what would I get for my subscription? And how much is a subscription?"

"Twelve hundred a year. For that you get an hour a week of peace and quiet and thoughtful reflection."

"No sermon?" Tucker asked.

"None."

"Any begging?" Attending church sometimes was like a PBS broadcast.

"Nope."

"No singing, dancing and holding hands?"

"Nope."

"And you could still go to your regular church if the need arose."

"If the need arose, you could. Attendance is not mandatory."

"You mean no one would be doomed to hell if they missed?"

"No."

"Where do I sign up?"

* * *

They were all sitting around the kitchen table. When Harry left he didn't take the kids with him so they were trying to work out some sleeping arrangements. It was decided that all the kids would sleep in the basement. The basement was finished and heated and one night of roughing it would be something the kids would like.

Marie was somewhat aggravated that Harry departed and left the kids.

"He could have waited till morning. It is not like he has to be somewhere."

Has to be in bed with his Internet babe Muldoon figured but didn't tell his sister that.

"Just gives you more ammunition," Cindy told her.

"I'm going to hang him. When I get through with him he is going to have that computer modem where the sun don't shine."

The kids had gone to the basement, but weren't sleeping. A lot of laughing and giggling going on. There were seven of them down there, so if they ever did get to sleep it would be a miracle

Frank was waiting for Father Harris to take him back to the rectory. His plane for the return trip to Rome would not leave till Sunday afternoon.

"It was a nice funeral," Emily said, "even though he didn't have a priest."

Frank shook his head. He would never hear the end of this.

"You know what I am going to do," she told him. "I am going to start a letter writing campaign."

Tom said, "What will that do?"

"You just watch and see," she told him. "I am going to get all the old Catholics in Florida to do it, and there are a lot of old Catholics in Florida."

"A lot of old everybody in Florida."

"Don't get smart. You watch and see. We will inundate the Bishops with letters wanting to know why the church can break a promise and not even care. And why are they so afraid of women?" Emily was now energized. Though now a widow her life now had direction and meaning. She was going to get some answers no matter what. And she would do it all in the memory of her husband, who deserved a priest.

The doorbell rang and it was Father Harris. Frank was actually glad to see him. Defending the church to your mother was a daunting task and one he wanted to avoid. He wasn't going to win it anyway.

Father Harris told Frank that he could celebrate the 5PM mass on Saturday and that would free him up to get ready for his return trip to Rome on Sunday.

"We can all go to that one," Emily announced.

"We plan to pull out before then," Marie informed everyone.

The evening moved along like that for a few more hours. Just idle talk. Frank did leave with Father Harris. Tom and Cindy went back to their motel. They were going to stay till Monday morning as Tom wanted to show Cindy some of his old haunts.

Around 11PM the kids had started to quiet down. Emily and Marie had gone to bed. Larry and Sarah were alone in their room for what seemed like the first time in a long time.

Larry told Sarah of Schmidt's removing the job offer of joining his agency.

"That didn't take long."

"It seems one of his kids came on some hard times so it leaves me out. So I guess Omaha may be it after all."

"Maybe next weekend we can go there and take a look around," Sarah said.

Larry thought that might be a good idea, but then he remembered Schwartz was coming to town on Monday so who knows what might happen. Neither he nor Sarah had much time to think or talk about Omaha.

He was sitting on the bed and she sat next to him. "So how you doing? You think your mother will be all right?"

"I'm sure she will be. She told me she would like to stay here a week, get a headstone and tie up some loose ends then return to Florida. I told her that would not be a problem. She has a good support group in Florida. She is probably better off there than here."

"What do you think of Cindy?" She asked him

"Nice looking. Smart. Seems a little suit happy, but I guess that is the lawyer in her."

"I think she might be good for Tom, and he might be good for her. She was very supportive of Marie and your mother. I like her."

"Until she sues you."

"They should go after Harry. The dope. Getting involved with some chicky on the Internet."

"Chicky?"

"Yeah, chicky. We all know that is not going to work. I hope Marie takes him to the cleaners."

Muldoon hadn't given it much thought. He always felt Harry was somewhat of a goof he simply wished his sister well.

"And I hope your mother starts that letter writing campaign. Wake up those old out of touch geezers that run the church."

"Geezers?"

"Yes geezers. And out of touch geezers."

Larry looked to Sarah and said, "You seemed to be as fired up as my mother."

"I feel sorry for her. You play by the rules and then when it comes your turn to get into the game the rules have been changed and no one has told you. I bet there are a lot of people like her out there."

362

"Probably," he was starting to feel tired. "I'm going to bed. I think this may be a long weekend." He kissed her on the cheek.

"Help your mother this week while she is here. The rest of the family will be gone, it will just be you and her, so be supportive."

"I thought I was," he said climbing under the covers.

"You are, but we all can do better," she said kissing him good night. "And I want a priest when I die."

"You could write a letter."

NINETEEN

Bosco pulled into the lot and saw Gladkowski's car parked near the door of his shop. The last thing Bosco did last night was call Gladkowski to talk about starting a church. Gladkowski was somewhat surprised to hear from him as he thought Bosco was off on his annulment kick and wouldn't be interested.

Plus the body shop business was becoming a pain in the ass, dealing with insurance adjusters, insurance companies, lawyers, whining customers, city inspectors. A church would be a nice quiet peaceful business to have. Just have to deal with the phony pious.

Gladkowski truly believed there was a need for a church devoted to only prayer and it would also present an easy opportunity to make a few bucks, as money and religion went hand in hand. He figured he would make some money and in the process might even save a soul. He was even more excited now that he might have Bosco on board. Gladkowski felt that for a church to be successful he would have to have someone with credentials.

Gladkowski had none.

Bosco had some.

Bosco was an ordained priest that got horny, but for whatever reason never lost his faith. Gladkowski as a youth was an altar boy went to Catholic grammar and high school but somewhere along the line simply drifted away. In a way he was kind of like Bosco but without the education.

Now to get back in the church's good graces even a guy like Gladkowski would have to do everything but die. Go to confession, spill your guts, be given a penance, sign up with a parish, go every Sunday, sell some raffle tickets or what most do, simply buy them so you don't have to sell them. You simply just couldn't go to Church to pray and begin over.

For one thing many were locked which kind of played hell with that sanctuary gambit. And then if you wanted to pray or just say a simple prayer, it had to be organized. God forbid you should pop in unannounced and pray.

"John, good morning to you." Gladkowski greeted Bosco. He shook his hand and welcomed Bosco as if he was the Prodigal Son returning. "Pull up a chair and have some coffee." There was no activity in the body shop. Occasionally they would work a half day on Saturday but they tried to avoid that whenever possible. The customer could always wait an extra day. Most of them expected it. It was when you finished a job early that they became concerned.

Bosco poured himself a cup and sat across from Gladkowski and didn't waste any time, "I think your church idea is a good one. My annulment deal is driving me nuts. First the cost, then a retreat and then god knows what? And I thought with my education, you know being a priest and all, I may be able to make something of this church idea."

This is pretty much what Gladkowski wanted to hear. It was as if Gladkowski had a pipeline to Bosco's brain. "That is good news John. Lot of people like you and me out there that just want to be able to pray without all the red tape."

"So what do we have to do to get started?" Bosco said. Bosco had decided after his phone call last night that he had to have a Plan B. Plan A was getting the annulment and then back into the

366

church's good graces. However the cost was becoming prohibitive and he knew from past experience there would be a lot of bullshit to put up with before anything would become final.

"First off," Gladkowski said, "we will need some seed money. So we may have to keep our little auto scam going for a while if for no other reason than for the honor and glory of God."

"Do you think that is really ethical? I would think a religion should start on some good solid ethics." Bosco's conscience was starting to bother him. He was all for getting back in church's good graces but he did feel one should be honest about it.

"This is a church for god's sake not some Ma and Pop type liquor store. If anyone would understand what we are doing here it would be organized religion. They know every scam under the sun. Don't go goofy on me now. We just have to do it till we have some money." Gladkowski was firm in making his feelings known.

All Bosco could say was, "How much?"

"Thirty thousand."

"Holy shit," Bosco said. "Why thirty thousand?" Bosco wondered if there was anything in religion that was cheap.

"Well," Gladkowski said leaning back in his chair. "We got to find a building to rent that is in a desirable location and in pretty good condition and maybe even looks like a church. Don't want some ratty old building. I figure that could take a while, and we would want to cap the rent at about one to two grand a month to start. Then we would have to church it up."

"Church it up?"

"Pews, kneelers, some religions pictures. Give it that old incense smell, candles, you know, the whole nine yards."

Bosco almost felt overwhelmed. Sounded to him that it could cost more than thirty grand.

"Plus we will have to advertise some."

"Advertise?"

"Well yeah, we got to get people in the doors. What do you think we just call a building a church open the doors and people make a bee line to us?" This Bosco might be educated but he is not too swift at times Gladkowski was thinking.

"What we can do for a starters is to get leaflets printed up and put them here and there." Gladkowski said.

"Here and there?"

"Yeah I'll put some in my body shops and will get Emanuel to put some out."

"You mean the guy over at your East Side location."

"Yeah."

"But he is black."

"So?"

"I want a nice safe white church."

Gladkowski was surprised by this. The last guy you would pick to have some prejudice in him would be someone that was educated in a seminary. But then again most religions despised queers.

"It's a church John. There is nothing happier than a black in prayer. Plus when they go to church they dress for church. Whites can learn from them when it comes to dressing for church. The ladies wear hats, men wear ties, and they pray their asses off."

"I thought this was going to be a nice quiet church?'

"Definitely."

"Blacks aren't quiet. They shout *Amen* at this and *Amen* at that, and *Praise the Lord* here, and *Lord have Mercy* there."

"We are going to tell them to pipe down." Gladkowski agreed. "It will be handled in our advertising. It will tell them to come to our church for an hour of quiet reflection. No church babble, if you get my drift?"

Bosco wasn't so sure. "What about Jews?"

Does this guy like anyone Gladkowski wondered? "What about them?"

"They can't be quiet for an hour."

"Excellent point." Gladkowski couldn't agree more. Jews had a tendency to get pushy and noisy. They think everything is discrimination. Worse than the blacks in that regard. Look at one cross-eyed and they are running off to the ACLU or some other goofy Jewish group whining their asses off.

"You know," Gladkowski told him, "if they could pray as well as they whine this would be a much better world. Well maybe they won't want to join. The fact that we will hold our prayer services on Sunday may discourage them or at the least cause them to whine. But they will be welcome. Perhaps we can have a no whining rule."

"We can only hope they understand." Then Bosco added, "what about Arabs and that ilk?"

Gladkowski looked at Bosco and wondered if he just wanted a place to go where he could be alone, as he seemed to be ruling everyone out. "Don't worry, they won't be there. They have their own churches or temples or whatever, and they are very cliquish. Plus no one is going to dress like they do, veils and towels and funny footwear.

"Funny footwear?"

"They have funny footwear take my word for it. They can come if they want," then he thought, "That too could be a rule, *no funny footwear*. Plus we are going to ask for money and they are cheaper than shit."

"I have also thought about the money end of it," Bosco said. "I was thinking about subscriptions." Bosco thought this was one great idea.

"Subscriptions?" This caused Gladkowski to raise an eyebrow. "You mean like a magazine?" He asked Bosco hesitatingly.

"More or less. I figure if we get the money up front it will give us working capital."

Gladkowski got up and walked over the coffeepot and poured himself a cup. He felt Bosco was starting to over think this church idea worrying about Blacks, Jews Arabs and now the money. By Gladkowski's standards this should be a pretty simple operation. Get them in the door then pass a basket. Let them say their little prayers or stare at the ceiling. Then wheel them out and bring in the next group. But then he didn't want to discourage Bosco as he figured having an ex-priest on board could only help and maybe subscriptions would be good, get money up front. Shit, now that he thought about it some churches use the Internet to get their cash. That would be the ultimate church just have them send money, don't even have to show up. I will have to look into that Gladkowski thought to himself.

"Well let's not worry about that right now John. Let's concentrate on getting our seed money and finding a location for the church. Keep your eyes open when you are driving about doing your claims work and check the papers. Once we get a building we can really begin to roll. Then he asked, "Are you still going for the annulment?"

"For now I am."

"Then we will need forty grand, ten for your annulment and thirty for our church. You should drop that annulment thing. It is nothing but hocus pocus anyway."

Bosco tended to agree but he wasn't ready to pull the plug yet. The Catholic guilt would kill him. "I got the ball rolling on it now and I want to see where it takes me."

"Like maybe heaven, eh?"

"Maybe." He smiled.

* * *

Marie, Emily and Sarah were looking at the Mass and condolence cards that were left at the funeral parlor. They were also paging through the guest book to see who was or wasn't at the wake and funeral. As far as they could tell everyone showed up except the Lloyds. The Lloyds were their neighbors for many years prior to their moving to Florida.

"Maybe they are dead?" Marie suggested.

"They're not dead," Emily said, "just lazy. They always like to tell you how busy they are. Don't have time for this or that. They're never busy they are just too lazy to do anything. Probably too lazy to come. But all in all it was a nice turnout."

Emily felt good about the turnout. If her husband had lived longer would have been less of a turnout. Kind of ironic the sooner you die the more mourners you have while the longer you live the less. Unfortunately that hospital did him in. She would have to go after them as well. Right after she got through with the church.

Muldoon was busy loading up Marie's rental for her return trip to Columbus. Marie was not happy about having to rent a car, but she had no choice as Harry went home alone with their car. Muldoon could sense that this would be another sticking point in their divorce, *the ass took the car and I had to ride home alone with the kids that should be worth a another grand a month your honor.*

Muldoon eventually got everything loaded and ready to go. Marie gave Sarah a hug, and her mother a hug and told her mother "to hang in there."

"What does that mean?"

"It means to hang in there, that you are not alone."

Emily simply shook her head as she thought the advice was stupid. "I suppose I could say the same to you. Maybe you will be able to work things out. Church frowns on divorce you know." She didn't know why she said that, it just came out. It just goes to show how Catholic guilt never leaves the system

"The church should get in the real world. Tell Frank I will stay in touch." She turned to Larry, "I don't suppose Tom and Cindy are going to be around."

Muldoon didn't know. Muldoon was waiting for her and her kids to leave so he could get on the computer and get some information about Omaha. That is all he wanted to do get on line and get some information about Omaha. But Marie's kids were on the computer all morning playing some stupid game, but now at long last they were headed for the door.

"Tell Cindy I will be in touch." She turned and instructed her kids to get in the car and get ready to leave. They all kissed and hugged their grandmother and then made their way to the car.

Larry stood outside near the drivers' side door as Marie got in.

"Good luck with Omaha," she said.

"Thanks, you too." He said absently.

"You never liked him anyway." She said. "Anyway I am going to be fine. You know why, I won't have a husband and of course the Church will disown me even though I am the one that got screwed over. I will truly be on my own. I couldn't be happier." She got in the car, checked the kids and started her drive to Columbus.

Muldoon watched her drive a way and thought that when she got to Columbus Harry was going to get an ear full.

"She is putting up a brave front." Sarah said.

"I don't think it is a front," Emily said. "She will be okay."

Muldoon was glad to see her and her kids finally leave.

Emily and Sarah continued to look through the guest book and cards while Muldoon made his way to the basement and the computer. But before he could get started he got a phone call from Joe Tucker.

"Missed you this morning," He said as Muldoon answered the phone.

"I don't come in on Saturdays remember."

"Well no one else did so don't feel bad."

"I won't."

"Hear the latest?"

Muldoon was afraid to ask but he did.

"The Reverend is starting a new church."

Muldoon wasn't sure if he heard correctly, "what do you mean?"

"I mean the Reverend is going to start a church of his own. And I think, just between you and me it might be a good idea."

"You are talking about Bosco, right?" Muldoon had a feeling this could be another one of those weird Tucker talks.

"Yeah. He says this annulment thing is becoming quite expensive so he has thought of starting his own."

Muldoon was speechless thinking about what he just heard. He had never known or heard of anyone starting a church, other than Martin Luther, who he only read about. He had no idea how you went about it. Did you have to be affiliated with another church?

"You still there?" Tucker asked.

"Yeah I'm here. I am just somewhat dumbfounded that's all."

"Going to be a church for prayer only." Tucker continued.

"Aren't they all?"

"No, you don't understand, here you just pray. No sermons, no nothing, just praying. And by the way your dad had a great idea on limiting sermons to seven minutes. He should be canonized for just having that brilliant idea."

"I'll pass it on."

"Yeah tell your brother Frank there in Rome perhaps he can get the ball rolling.

"Getting back to Bosco what's he going to do?" Muldoon found this hard to believe. After all Bosco in his own strange way seemed pretty devoted to getting back in the church's good graces, but perhaps the price was getting a bit steep. Ten grand was a lot of money not to mention the two month retreat. He thought Frank made that part up. Muldoon had yet to talk to Frank about it. He made a mental note to do that before Frank left. He didn't really care but you wouldn't think the church would be so hard nosed over things they had no control.

Tucker repeated the story about the church, the no sermon rule, the no singing, and no raffle rules. Just a place to go once a week to plop and pray. "Yeah Larry," Tucker concluded, "I think the Reverend is on to something. I might even join. We have a real windbag for a pastor. Not having to listen to him on Sundays would be like dying and going to heaven."

"Thanks for the information." Was all Muldoon could say.

"No problem. I think if we can get in on the ground floor on something like this we can be saints."

"I don't think it is that simple." Muldoon said.

"Hell now they are running them through like pouring piss out of a boot. Just have to die and start a letter writing campaign I think."

Muldoon could tell that Tucker was starting to drift, and the letter writing campaign made him think of his mother. He ended the conversation thanking Tucker for the news and told him he would see him on Monday for the meeting with Schwartz.

TWENTY

Muldoon had no idea on where the time was going. Here it was Sunday afternoon and he was just getting on line to get some information about Omaha. It was half time during the Bear game and they were losing 28-3. Still no quarterback. October and the team was already demoralized. Only thing worse than having no quarterback was listening to talk radio whine about it forever. He was glad he commuted to work and wasn't exposed to that drivel on a daily basis. But then again he imagined Omaha would have that.

Probably whine about the Nebraska Cornhuskers all day long. No place was perfect.

Yesterday when he got off the phone with Tucker he started thinking, actually daydreaming about Bosco and his church and then before he knew it it was time for 5 o'clock mass. He felt that Bosco having his own little church might not be a bad idea. Hell, it couldn't be worse than working in insurance. At least with a church you knew whom you were working for.

They all went to mass and Frank celebrated it, and he kept his sermon short. He had obviously paid attention to the eulogy. The congregation seemed quite pleased. Tom and Cindy showed up though Cindy was not Catholic. However she was a good sport and went along for the sake of Emily and probably figuring there might be a chance for her to sue a Florida hospital. Most lawyers felt sucking up to a potential plaintiff was a good business practice.

Then they all went out to dinner at a Greek restaurant where you could get a drink with a meal, which according to Emily was as important as the meal. Emily did not care for family restaurants, as you could not always get a drink. Maybe some cheap wine but not a good hard drink. *A little booze to chase your blues,* as she liked to say.

Now everyone was upstairs watching the Bears go down the toilet while Tom wondered why they weren't playing the World Series. Last night's game was cancelled due to rain in New York though according to the broadcasters and the reports in the paper the weather was perfect during the day. Did not turn lousy till about forty-five minutes to game time. Then a cold downpour for over three and a half hours.

"I don't know why they can't play during the day for god's sake," Tom said. "What will happen if they play day games on the weekends? Is college football going to be set back 50 years? And why can't they play on Sunday? The NFL can just move their games back to late starts. Major League baseball hates the Major League fan." He concluded.

"So why are you becoming an umpire?" Frank asked him

"To save the game for the common fan like our dad."

No one could disagree with that. If the game got rained out on Sunday they might not finish the World Series till after Christmas.

"You got mail." The computer said.

Muldoon looked and most was gibberish though the price of Viagra did appear to be going down. Muldoon thought that perhaps by the time he needed it it would be so cheap he could pop them like candy. Keep all the ladies alert. There was an email from Marie informing everyone that she and the kids arrived safe and sound and that she would be in touch. She did not mention Harry.

According to the Internet Omaha has a population of 390,000 plus. Creighton University is there, not to mention Boys Town and Offutt Air Force Base and the Strategic Air Command. They play the College World Series there in weather appropriate for baseball. Warren Buffet spends his money there, Forbes magazine lists it as one of the 15 best places to live and *Parenting* magazine lists it in the Top 10 places to raise kids. The entire state of Nebraska has only 1.7 million people and one third of the jobs in Omaha are service jobs. Right up Muldoon's alley. The winters average 32 inches of snow. Mutual of Omaha is there, the company that sponsored that animal show everyone talked about, the one with the anaconda. The real estate prices he checked seemed okay, but that was something you had to do in person. They could make anything sound and look nice on the Internet.

Omaha sounded like a pretty nice place. Muldoon now wondered what would screw it up?

He then checked the *New York Times* web site to see what Maureen Dowd was upset about, mainly Republicans and the Catholic hierarchy. Muldoon thought it was a shame she didn't know Bosco as he was just nuts enough to be part of the hierarchy, except for the marriage and divorce part.

He then checked the book section but nothing seemed interesting there. The *Times* goes through phases where they refuse to review anything someone might actually read and this Sunday appeared to be one of those phases. Muldoon enjoyed reading book reviews of books that interested him, but nothing grabbed his interest.

When he returned to the game it was almost over and the Bears were now down 38-13. Bear fans would interpret this as "well we played even with them in the second half".

All the ladies were in the kitchen, Emily, Sarah and Cindy sitting around the kitchen table, bonding time. They were laughing and having fun talking about this and that while sipping wine. Cindy was telling them all about growing up in Paradise, California. She was going on about Johnny Appleseed Days and how all present should make the trip to Paradise for that occasion. And of course if they came San Francisco was only 175 miles away and they would have to go there as well. It would be a great time.

"What's for dinner?" Muldoon asked.

"Corn beef and cabbage, and don't lift the lid," his mother told him.

It was his father's favorite meal and it smelled good. Muldoon left the ladies and returned to the game. It had just ended and the Bears had gone down to defeat. They all walked off the field as if they were just told they had a dose of the clap.

Frank was sitting in the recliner. He had plans to take an early flight but Father Harris found better connections for him. Though the flight was later and he had less time between connections. Frank was wearing his non-priest outfit, Dockers and a sweater. No Roman collar. Tom was on the couch working the remote looking for the weather channel to find the weather for New York and the World Series game that night.

The twins who started watching the game left when it got out of hand, about three minutes into the first quarter, now returned and wanted to know the final. When told they left again. Their sister Emily was at a friend's house.

"Look at that, rain is predicted for New York." Tom said. "I bet it has been nice all day." He flipped back to see highlights of the early football games and sure enough the highlights of the Giants game came on. They played in New York and the sun was shining.

"This is pathetic, baseball sucks" he said. "Where did the boys go? Maybe we can toss a football or around." He got up and left.

Larry and Frank were alone when Muldoon looked to his brother who did appear that he was thinking of napping, "Why does an annulment cost money?" Muldoon asked. He hadn't had much of a chance to talk to Frank since here, and there were better things to talk about than annulments but still Muldoon wanted to know.

"Don't start."

"What do you mean 'don't start'. It is a simple question."

"Nothing is free." He said placing the recliner in an almost prone position hoping his brother would talk about something else.

"All you have to do is sign a piece of paper. How can that cost $10,000? And why does he need one anyway?" Muldoon couldn't believe he was actually defending Bosco.

"Because a full sacramental marriage never took place," Frank said calmly. Frank decided instead of getting upset and arguing the issue he would speak in rational tones and eventually the subject would go away or be changed.

"Bunch of Catholic gobblygook. What difference does it make where someone got married?"

Frank let out a sigh. "You know you are your mother's son." Larry took this as a compliment. "

The Church believes," Frank said, "and you may not agree, that it has the fullest understanding of what a sacramental marriage is and the right to make judgments about the sacramental status of any Christian marriage."

What a mouthful Muldoon thought. "If they showed as much concern for the sexual abuse of minors as they do about their miss guided morality on the sanctity of marriage we all would be better off."

Frank had no response. In a way he agreed with his brother but then he was a priest and did feel somewhat of an obligation to defend the church. He often wondered how the church allowed themselves to get in this position. He was glad to be in Rome where sins of the church were largely ignored.

"You know he is thinking of starting his own church as the one he loves is screwing him over."

This bit of news perked up Frank, "he is going to start his own church? He is not a Bishop he can't ordain any priests."

"I don't know about all that. It sounds like he just wants to go to a place to pray without a lot of baggage and try to follow his true vocation in life, which he believes is in the religious field."

"Then he shouldn't have gotten married and left the church. Anyway you can pray anywhere. You don't need a church. How many Bear fans do you think prayed today for a victory?"

"Obviously not enough."

"Maybe so, but they all didn't do it in church. They did it sitting on their couch or easy chair with a beer in one hand and a remote in the other. You don't need a church to pray. The trouble is everyone wants it easier. Everyone wants the easy way out. They want the gain but not the pain.

"Your friend wanted to get married as that was convenient at the time. But now that that didn't work he wants back in and for some reason we are simply to throw open our doors. How do we know he won't change his mind again? He is unhappy and now we are supposed to give him the easy way out."

"That is the same old song and dance we always hear." Muldoon said. "Like it is some kind of badge of honor to be allowed to suffer for god or whatever. Like we all should look forward to a little suffering, but in Bosco's case he has to pay and probably jump through a few hoops. I bet god would be happy if more people went to a church to pray than sitting on their asses in front of the TV praying for a dumb football game."

"Well it is obvious that god is not a Bear fan. You would think Bear fans would have figured that out by now." Frank said trying to lighten up the discussion.

"What is this 60 day retreat?" Muldoon couldn't let up. The 60-day retreat deal sounded as pathetic as the money grab.

"For God's sake the guy was a priest, quit, got married, got divorced, and wants back in. We just supposed to throw open the doors to him."

"What about the Prodigal Son?"

"He just wasted part of his life goofing off and chasing women."

"And that is the easy road?"

Frank let out a sigh. "I don't know who gets what. All I tried to do was be honest with your friend. Though the 60-day retreat was my idea," Frank actually liked that idea. Figured that would be a good test as to whether someone really did want to get back in. Anyone can buy their way in. Just need a check and a sorrowful attitude. "Anyway can't we talk about something else? Between you and Mom and her nine First Fridays you're going to drive me nuts."

"Well they should do something about that as well. Making promises, not keeping them and then just pretending the promise was never made."

"Who?"

"Never mind."

Frank just shook his head and closed his eyes. He should have taken the early flight.

*   *   *

The corn beef and cabbage was excellent. Cindy had never had it before and was quite pleased. Muldoon even had a 6 pack of Guinness they all shared with dinner, with the exception of the kids. Everyone agreed there is nothing better than a good boiled meal.

During coffee Cindy excitedly said, "Guess what? You will never guess what I did today."

No one could.

"This morning I got up. Sat on the bed. Looked to the heavens and said, 'The Cubs Suck' and immediately I felt better."

"The truth will set you free."

* * *

Bosco was sitting looking at the paper. He was reading the real estate ads looking for a church to buy. He was going to go out and drive around and look at some, but most of the ads did not have an address just a general area where it was located and he didn't want to talk to some real estate guy. He did not come across any churches for sale but there was commercial property that might serve the need. For now the problem was the money. Their little auto damage-padding scheme was just getting off the ground and it could take some time to come with money for both the annulment and the church.

Eventually he was also going to have to approach Sheila and break the news to her that he was going to get their marriage annulled. He had been putting that off. He wanted to wait until the divorce was final and then drop that on her. She would probably go ballistic just for the sake of aggravating him. But telling her he was going to have their marriage annulled would aggravate her. This was one of the reasons they were getting divorced; they loved aggravating each other.

He was going to call Gladkowski but decided not to. Bosco did like the church idea but he also knew somewhere along the line he would have to preach or at least counsel some poor sinner. You just can't pray all the time. Gladkowski did have a good idea about a church for prayer only but eventually they would have to have a service with a sermon on occasion. He felt he could convince Gladkowski that that would make the church more viable. Simply have two or three prayer services each Sunday where people could just come and plop and pray, but then one service with some preaching. Some church members might need a little direction, and Bosco felt no one better than him to give it.

He started to watch the Bear game but three minutes into the first quarter they were already losing 14-0. They fumbled the opening kickoff and then Detroit ran two simple running plays and had a touchdown. Detroit then kicks off. Bears manage not to fumble but then on their third play from scrimmage throw an interception. This time one pass and two simple running plays result in a touchdown. They then showed a shot of the Bear sideline and all the players looked like they were just told they had the clap. What a dismal looking group of athletes Bosco thought. He turned it off as they were just depressing him

It was then that he started searching the paper. He circled a couple of ads he saw that looked promising and would try to call tomorrow. He remembered Schwartz was going to be in the office in the morning, and though he would be here mainly for underwriting Bosco felt he should put in an appearance for appearances sake. People who thought they were important like to be treated that way though Bosco thought Schwartz was a hopeless loser.

He had met Schwartz once before and Schwartz asked him, "and what do you do in claims?"

Bosco looked at him and Schwartz had a look like he honestly didn't know. The guy was a vice president of an insurance company and looked as if his brain had checked out about three to four years ago. At first Bosco didn't answer as he thought the guy was kidding but he stood there waiting for an answer.

Bosco looked over to Vicki who was shuffling some papers on her desk which was the first and last time Bosco could remember Vicki doing anything that resembled work. He then looked at Schwartz and said, "We settle them."

Schwartz went, "hmmmm" and then walked away.

Bosco figured if all went according to plan, next year at this time he would be back in the church's good graces or preaching on his own and Schwartz would be visiting some office wondering "exactly what is insurance?"

* * *

Everyone had left. Joe and Cindy were going to head back to California but reminded everyone that they had plans to get married around Thanksgiving and were hoping all could show up in Vegas where the wedding would take place.

Frank heard this but kept quiet. He felt his brother should get married in the church but he knew this was not the time to bring it up. Anyway Frank wanted to get back to Rome. He knew he would be in Rome for their wedding and had no intention to come back for something like that. He simply shook his brother's hand, gave Cindy a peck on the cheek and wished them both the best.

Father Harris would take him to the airport. He gave his mother a hug and told her he would keep her in his prayers and think about her often, and try to get back to the states soon.

"Thank you Frank," she had said, "But you should probably pray for the church and find out why they are so screwed up as I am going to start my letter writing campaign."

He could only smile. If nothing else it would keep her going and he liked the thought of that.

"This has been quite a week," Sarah said to Larry when they were alone in their room. Emily and the kids were in bed. The house was quiet.

"A lot has happened" He agreed. "A possible move to Omaha. A job offer from an insurance agency and a job offer removed from that agency. My father's death and burial. My mother's rage against the church for not having a priest with my father when he was dying even though he made the Nine First Fridays. Bosco and his annulment plea to Frank."

"Don't forget Cindy," she reminded him. "You know she is going to sue somebody."

"I think that might be in her blood."

"We should try to make their wedding. There are usually cheap flights out to Vegas and it would be fun. And you know she will make a pretty bride."

He agreed. He then told her about looking up Omaha on the Internet and that it looked like a nice place to live. "After my mother returns to Florida we should make it a point to go there and if all goes well perhaps we can work in a trip to Vegas."

"How soon do you think before we will have to decide about Omaha?"

"I don't know. This guy Schwartz is coming tomorrow to talk to underwriting, so I hope to have better information then."

"Who is he?"

"Some VP. I don't know exactly they have a VP for practically every day of the year. He could be here with good news or bad news or just making the rounds for something to do."

Sarah got in bed while Larry sat at the foot of it. He felt tired. A long week. He enjoyed seeing his family but naturally wished it was under different circumstances. He had the feeling with everyone scattered about they would see each other rarely and probably not all together again until another death or when one of his kids got married which hopefully was good 12-15 years away.

Finally he crawled into bed gave Sarah a kiss and they immediately fell asleep.

TWENTY ONE

Tucker arrived at the office before 7AM. This was the earliest he that he had ever been to work in his entire life. He figured by getting to the office early by the time Schwartz arrived he would have a 50-50 chance of being alert. When the Home Office suits showed up Tucker did feel an obligation of sorts to be alert. Home Office types tended to think that was important. His wife told him he had nothing to worry about. She even got up early with him to fix him a little breakfast and send him on his way with a good luck kiss.

In the lobby of the building he picked up a 15-cent cup a coffee and was charged $4.50 for it. What a racket cups of coffee had become. He brought the coffee as he knew that Wanda, the dip in charge of clerical, would not be in this early and there would be no coffee in the office, and god forbid if someone touched her coffeepot.

He entered the office tuned on the lights and made his way to his office located in the corner. He had no idea when Schwartz was going to show. Usually the suits would stay at the Omni Hotel off of North Michigan and then make their way to the office around 9AM. They liked to make a grand entrance.

He assumed Schwartz got in last night made his way over to Rush Street maybe even had dinner at Harry Caray's Restaurant. Tucker knew that when they traveled they believed in spending money. Then the first thing they would talk about would be how we have to control expenses. Executives were such frauds.

The reason Tucker came in early, other than trying to be alert, was he wanted to try and figure on what would happen during the day. Usually when these guys traveled there would be good news or bad news, sometimes both. Tucker wanted to be prepared for any eventuality though he was beginning to get to the point in his life where he simply didn't care. He still had to give the impression that he did.

Tucker entered his office and his desk was spotless. No papers, no files piled on it. All that was there was his phone, a desk calendar, a picture of his wife a couple of other family pictures and a yellow legal pad for taking notes, though he rarely took notes.

He was sipping his coffee and thought it tasted like ordinary coffee. He felt that for $4.50 he should have gotten something that tasted a lot better than this. The coffee they made at home was better than this. He could only figure that the people in Seattle had their taste buds up their ass.

He then saw Bosco walk in. He too was early. Tucker made his way over

"Good morning Reverend. I just want to tell you I think that church idea you have is a good one."

Bosco was surprised. "Thanks."

"Here early."

"I thought with Schwartz coming in perhaps I should be here." Bosco like most employees everywhere felt you should always try to cover your ass. He had no idea on what Schwartz was going to be doing today other than meet with the underwriters but by being present and also looking alert it couldn't hurt.

"Perhaps you could sell him on that church idea," Tucker suggested, then thought for a second and said, "You know I went to church yesterday. Eight o'clock mass. Went to that one as I wanted to get home, have a nice breakfast, and watch some of the Sunday talk shows then watch the Bears. But this priest we have went on and on about something I don't know exactly what. He babbled on for fifteen to twenty minutes and managed to say absolutely nothing.

"I tell you I looked around the church, checking out the other people, no one was paying attention. Two people were actually sleeping. I thought with this idea you have I could pop in on a Sunday at eight say my prayers, do my reflecting, and be on my merry way. All that guy did yesterday was aggravate everyone."

Bosco listened and knew Tucker was right. Bosco remembered when he was a priest. Some Sundays you simply didn't have anything prepared to talk about so you would wing it. And when you tried to wing it you could really drone on. The sermon would be so stupid and boring you wouldn't even be listening to yourself and really get confused. That is why he thought this church idea was good. The idea was so simple it was good. He wanted to preach, but he wanted to give good sermons. When you prepare them and give them from the heart, and don't read them they can be pretty good. But there was also a time for prayer and reflection and peace and quiet. He couldn't believe that someone like Gladkowski could come up with such a simple and profound idea.

Could revolutionize Christianity.

"Did you watch the game?" He asked Bosco."

"No, I was busy." He didn't feel it was necessary to tell Tucker about the start of the church hunt.

"Well you didn't miss a thing. You know the great thing about them losing is now we no longer have to screw up our

Sundays watching them. They're out of it. Some of those morons on the radio think they can still get in the playoffs. They must get paid to be stupid. Like, so what? Get in the playoffs, play one game and lose. Nothing exciting about that."

Bosco was wondering why Tucker was jabbering so. This is the most Tucker had talked to him in he didn't know how long. Maybe it was because Schwartz was coming in and he had some nervous energy to burn off.

Slowly the office started to fill up. All the men talked about the horrible Bear game and all the women just talked about Nate Berkus and his latest decorating ideas or Rachel Ray and what you can or can't cook in 30 minutes.

Then at 9 AM David Schwartz made his entrance. He had a raincoat, though it was sunny out, which he hung in a closet off the reception area and made his way back to Tucker's office slowly walking past the cubicles. He was wearing a blue pin stripe suit with crisp white shirt and his head was shaved. He was six feet tall, a solid 190 pounds. Most avoided eye contact with him as no one wanted him to stop at their cubicle and chat, or have him ask something about what they did. VPs like to ask people that work under them what they do. Perhaps they think they will hear something profound.

"Good morning Joe."

Tucker saw him walk in and walk back to the office but Tucker picked up his phone and pretended to be on it as Schwartz entered his office.

"I will get back to you as soon as I can." He hung up the phone, "Hi David good to see you," he said getting up out of his chair and extending his hand. Then he noticed that Schwartz had an earring. He stared at it. Looked like a diamond. What ear was it in? He is facing me and the earring is on my right so that must be his left ear. Damn, I knew I should have gotten my ear pierced was all Tucker could think. Shaved head too. This guy Schwartz could be someone to watch.

"Like some coffee?" Tucker asked.

"Yes, that would be nice. Black."

Tucker asked his secretary to have Wanda, the dip in charge of clerical, to bring a cup of black coffee to his office. They made some small talk until Wanda returned with the coffee with a put upon look on her face. Before Wanda could start in on how she wasn't a waitress and had better things to do than deliver coffee Tucker said. "Wanda I would like you to meet our Vice President, David Schwartz."

This had the desired affect. Caught Wanda off guard as she was rarely introduced to people. She simply handed the coffee to Schwartz he thanked her and she then casually exited the office.

Schwartz who was now sitting in a chair facing Tucker took a sip of coffee, set the cup on the desk and looked at Tucker and said, "Might as well get right to work, send in Richards."

Tucker drew a blank.

Who was Richards?

He looked to Schwartz hoping for a clue but Schwartz had a briefcase open on his lap and was going through some papers.

Tucker looked past Schwartz out to the office trying to place the name with a face, but everyone was in their cubicle out of sight.

"Isn't he here today?"

There was a clue, it's a he. "I just have to go out and have Emma track him down." Emma was his secretary.

He asked her to get Richards and a few minutes later Bernie entered the office.

* * *

Sarah showed Emily the computer and some of the ins and outs of using it. Emily was familiar with computers from the one they had in Florida. She wanted to write the first draft of her letter to the church while it was all fresh in her mind, and she thought of no better time to start than now.

Dear Reverend. She started. She was going to start with *Your Holiness* but then figured the Pope wouldn't get involved until she really rocked the boat. *My dear sweet husband passed away recently. A hospital did him in though that is not a concern of yours at this time but if you ignore me it might be.* She had no idea what that meant but a threat here and there felt good. After all the Church spent most of their waking hours dooming everyone to Hell or Purgatory might as well get a few licks in while she could.

My husband had made the Nine First Fridays several dozen times and even the Five First Saturdays as we were told many times over that making the Nine First Fridays entitled one to a Happy Death and a priest. He had neither. I want to know why?

*I am not saying he was unhappy but he would have been a lot happier with a priest and so **will** I.*

As you may know my son is a priest assigned to Rome and he had no answer for this horrible omission. I have a new friend, a lawyer, and the consensus is you owe one of us dearly.

Unfortunately my husband, now deceased, cannot accept any payment for your dismal failure to keep your promise. However I am alive and well and can accept whatever you have to offer.

We expect more than a written apology, more than a Novena, more than some prayers for the dead. We expect compensation. Emily didn't know what type of compensation she would receive, if any, as she never thought of compensation till just now when she typed it. But it sounded like one great idea.

*I know you have a lot of sexual abused people to pay off; however that is not my problem. Your paranoia about sex brought some of that on. You could change that paranoia by letting some women in as you men have bungled things long enough. It is a crime what men are doing to Holy **Mother** the Church. You noted I highlighted mother. Hopefully you smart men can figure out why.*

You may say you have changed these rules when you defrocked some saints like the wonderful St. Christopher. Well not for me and my husband. Remember there are four things to remember before dying, Death, Judgment, Heaven and Hell. If you don't want three of the four to come down on you you will figure a way to make good on your promise.

I am looking forward to your response. If not received soon, you will hear from my friends and me again and again and again and again and again, Amen.

Emily read it and thought not bad for a first draft. Might perk them up some. She didn't know how St. Christopher got involved but she wanted to let them know she knew all the saints, active and inactive. She didn't know if any of the rules had changed, but in case they had she wanted to give the impression she was up to date. Perhaps it would make them think though then again that could well be an impossible task.

* * *

Bernie came out of the office no worse for wear. He walked over to Doris Simpson's cubicle and said, "They want to see you."

No sooner had Bernie arrived at his cubicle than Muldoon, Robinson and Phillips were there. "What happened?"

"They asked me to go to Omaha?"

"What?" Muldoon said. His mind was racing, how the hell can that be?

Both Robinson and Phillips were somewhat surprised by this.

Trevayne turned to Muldoon and said, "You just can't trust the white man. Here you is about to uproot your family and they offer the job to Bernie."

"Man that does suck." Phillips agreed.

"Not as underwriting manager," Bernie said, "but as an underwriting supervisor, a demotion."

"You have to go to Omaha to get demoted? That doesn't sound fair." Phillips figured why couldn't they screw over Bernie right here. You shouldn't have to send someone to Omaha to screw them over.

What the hell is going on thought Muldoon? If he went to Omaha it would be to get away from goofs like Bernie. To go to

Omaha and be Bernie's boss could present problems. Muldoon should have figured this was not going to be easy. CMI would do something to screw things up and sure enough they were.

"You going?" Phillips asked.

Muldoon looked at Bernie to hear what he had to say. "Screw-em, I gave them the old song and dance that I would have to talk it over with my wife, but fuck-em. I am not going to Omaha. As soon as I can I'm going to a headhunter and see what is out there."

"That's the spirit," Trevayne said. "Don't let them push you around." But Trevayne and everyone knew they were putting the screws to Bernie to get rid of him.

Phillips was listening to all this, "Wait a minute," he said. "If you leave, and Robinson here ready to vacate, and Muldoon going to Omaha and Roundtree god knows where what the hell is going to become of this office? I can't do it all."

"Looks like you may have to end those naps." Bernie said.

"Bullshit. No point in working if you can't nap."

"And people say we loaf." Robinson said.

"Loafing and sleeping are two different things."

Just then Emma entered their group, "Larry they want to see you now."

Muldoon looked at Emma and she simply shrugged and walked back to her desk.

Muldoon started the walk to Tucker's office. He had been there many times in the past but suddenly it seemed like a long walk. He felt all the eyes in the office watching him make this pilgrimage. All he could think was this could be the beginning or the end or the end of the beginning.

He entered and was greeted by Schwartz. Doris was gone; where she had disappeared to he did not know. He shook Schwartz's hand while wondering what happened to Doris. Tucker sat there as if completely oblivious rubbing an ear lobe.

"Good to see you Larry," It was then Muldoon noted the earring or piercing or whatever you call it when the VP of the company is trying to keep his youth. He looked to Tucker who was rubbing his left lobe and now smiling.

"Have a seat."

Muldoon did as told.

"Larry we have some good news, don't we Joe." Schwartz said speaking to Muldoon while looking at Tucker for support.

"We do?" Tucker asked.

Muldoon and Schwartz looked to Tucker. "Yes we do," Tucker quickly added. "Wonderful news."

"Larry, we would like you to be the Underwriting Manager of our Chicago office."

All went quiet. Tucker and Schwartz were looking to Muldoon waiting for a response. Muldoon wasn't sure what he had just heard and for a moment he tried to figure out where the Chicago office was.

Then it dawned on him. They mean here, where I am. Don't have to move.

"Yes Larry, this is a great opportunity for you." It was Tucker

Then Muldoon thought I'll still be here with Tucker. That was a mind boggling proposition.

"Yes Larry," Schwartz said. "This is a great opportunity." They speak alike Muldoon thought.

"But I just talked to Bernie and he may be leaving, Robinson is leaving and Roundtree is…." Then Muldoon stopped short. He didn't know if Schwartz knew about Roundtree missing in action. He looked to Tucker, but Tucker looked unconcerned.

"What about Roundtree?" Schwartz asked.

"Oh he is on vacation," Tucker said. "Went to South America. He is kind of burned out. But when he returns he'll be as good as new. Needed some bonding time with his son. You know the kid," Tucker spoke in very confidential tones, "wants to become a lawyer."

"Good god in heaven, like we need another lawyer!" Schwartz said. "How sad and depressing to hear that. That is horrible news. An offspring wanting to become a lawyer. And by the way Larry sorry to hear about your dad."

"He gave his own eulogy," Tucker said.

"I thought he was dead."

Muldoon took a quick look around the office. I'm stuck in here with two idiots. "He wrote it before he died and my sister read it."

Schwartz thought about that. "Sounds like a good idea. Surprised more people don't do that."

"They will now. His eulogy is the home of the 7 minute sermon." Tucker said pleased with himself for coming up with the phrase *home of the 7-minute sermon.* He liked the sound of it. Now if he could get that guy from yesterday to buy into it the world indeed would be a better place to live.

Schwartz didn't pursue it but went back to the original subject "Well Larry," he said, "we are not going to leave you high and dry. Doris will be on board. We are making her an underwriting supervisor of both property and casualty. And you will be Underwriting Manager of both property and casualty."

"Sounds like duplication."

"On the surface it does," Schwartz agreed while readjusting himself in his seat. "But this is a great new concept we have come up with. It is called *Corporate Efficiency*. You see you will manage and Dorothy will supervise. It won't be broken into property and or casualty manager or supervisor. One manager, one supervisor for the whole shebang. Very efficient thus the name *Corporate Efficiency*."

Muldoon listened but didn't hear anything because Schwartz wasn't saying anything that made sense. A manager and a supervisor with basically the same titles, doing the same thing. *Corporate Efficiency?* Sounded so stupid it could work "Compensation?"

"That's the best part; you get a raise, 20%. We are going to get a replacement for Trevayne." Then he looked to Tucker, "I suppose he wants an exit interview?"

"He wants that more than anything." Tucker said. "Actually he is living for the day he has it."

"Blacks," he looked to Muldoon hoping he didn't offend him, "you're not a racial nut are you Larry?"

"I don't consider myself nuts in any way shape or form."

"Good. But Blacks and their damn exit interviews. They think we actually give a shit what they think when they leave. We don't care what anyone thinks when they leave. We don't care if you're white, black, gay, straight, male, female, young or old. If you decide to leave us we could care less what you think. But some ass in Human Resources somewhere said this is a good tool. A good tool for some useless worker to vent. Not that Trevayne was useless, he has been a faithful and productive employee, but we don't give a shit about his petty crap.

"That being said you will have to hire a smoke to replace him. I know you have some here in Loss Control, and you have that auditor here Jesse Smith, but none in underwriting. We could transfer one here, but we got to keep expenses under control, so we will have to go out and find one. Should not be a problem."

"When does all this take place?" Muldoon asked.

"Now. No point in waiting. When you come in tomorrow you will be the Underwriting Manager. We move fast, that is *Corporate Efficiency* in action."

Muldoon wondered about Bernie. Muldoon knew Bernie wasn't going to go to Omaha to be demoted. But then if he was going to be a supervisor and not a manger maybe he wasn't being promoted. Who the hell knew? *Corporate Efficiency* sound like a mind-boggling proposition. What Bernie would do is hang on for a while. Tell them he is thinking it over so they keep him on. Look for a job and fuck things over when the opportunity arose. Muldoon didn't know if he should rat Bernie out. He didn't want his first executive decision to be ratting someone out. He thought Bernie was useless, but he was still a decent person. Muldoon decided to keep quiet figured what the hell, could blame it on the transition.

"The great news Larry," Tucker told him, "is you have Doris on board. She is bright, though somewhat plain looking. She will be a good person to lean on."

Muldoon was wondering what happened to Doris? She came here for her meeting and then gone. He wanted to talk to her to make sure she wasn't expecting this job and might have some bitterness in her. And why do they think I have to lean on her?

There was a knock on Tucker's door and Vicki entered looking distraught. "I just got a call. Roundtree is dead."

Tucker and Muldoon looked at each other than back to Vicki.

"An anaconda killed him," she said. "He was on some expedition in South America and he got squeezed to death."

Both Tucker and Muldoon were dumbfounded and then Tucker said, "He should have had a cameraman in the bush like Marlin."

At least we won't have to give him an exit interview Tucker then thought to himself.

Muldoon couldn't believe what he just heard. Roundtree dead. He had worked next to Roundtree for over 4 years. And now killed by a snake. Who would think an underwriter would be killed by a snake? What were the odds of that happening? Sounded as if the snake knew something about *corporate efficiency*

"Did the snake eat him? They swallow people whole you know?" Tucker saw that on the Animal Channel. Snakes swallow things whole, amazing.

"I don't know," Vicki said turning to leave.

They watched her walk away. "Man, she is one good looking woman," Schwartz said. "Wouldn't mind having her squeeze the life out of me."

They both looked at Schwartz thinking that that remark was insensitive, but then again quite true.

"Maybe we should take a break," Tucker said. "I'm sure once the news about Roundtree gets through the office people will feel bad, as well they should."

"Christ an anaconda, who would have ever thought."

TWENTY TWO

Emily was still at the computer. She played some solitaire and free cell. She even thought of going on line but didn't know what she would do once she did. Sarah had called down to her that she was going to run up to the store and did she want to come along. Emily decided to stay where she was and have some time by herself.

This was the first time she was really alone since her husband died. The other night she had a good cry and now this was really the first time she had time to think. She knew that a bit of her died with her husband but she made up her mind that she was not going to become a slug. She was going to live her life as best she could and not go through the remainder of her life feeling sorry for herself. She had many friends in Florida who would help and she had her children and she had wonderful memories. There was no reason to mope.

She re-read the letter she wrote to the Church and thought it was pretty good. She thought perhaps she should write another one on Marie's behalf. She felt for her daughter. A divorce was not good, but a Catholic getting one was Hell on earth. Marie was only 40 years old and still had a full life to live, but due to the idiocy of the Church she may not remarry unless she lied and told the Church how sorry she was to be rid of the fornicator when in truth she wouldn't be. Emily hoped that when the divorce was final Marie would be a full woman not worrying about stupid restrictions put on her by a bunch of senile old men. Why should anyone be penalized for the sins of their spouse? That is guilt by association. The day would come Emily figured that the Church would get religion and learn the errors of its ways. All what was needed was some women in leadership roles. A woman priest would be a worthy goal of the Church. Kind of like putting a man on the moon was for this country

She enjoyed seeing Tom and Cindy. They did seem happy together and Cindy was full of life. Emily would definitely go out to California to visit with them. Perhaps she could even make their wedding in Las Vegas another marriage the Church would frown on. Why should they care where two people who love each other get married?

Emily could not imagine such paranoia. The Church made it sound that a Catholic not getting married in the Church was leading a life of sin. She doubted very much that at the Final Judgment the Lord would be there and say *well Tom and Cindy you had a long successful marriage, faithful to each other, honest. Did a wonderful job raising your children. You showed them much love and affection. The world was a bit better place when the two of you became one. Unfortunately you did not get married in the Church so you are going to have to burn for a while.* No one could believe that. In Florida she knew a lot of happily married couples and all were not married in the Church. She also knew some unhappy ones that were. And she knew some, old as she, who simply lived with someone and still very moral. Like to see the Church explain that.

She felt good about her children. Frank the priest who wanted to make the world a better place for everyone. Marie their only daughter, who may be going through a difficult time but no doubt, would come out on top. Tom who found a nice, smart, attractive woman, and a lawyer to boot and who soon would be a Major League Umpire assuming this year's World Series ended before the start of the next season. And of course Larry and Sarah. Larry was so much like his dad it was scary and Emily liked to think that perhaps Sarah had a bit of her in her but that was probably wishful thinking. They may go to Omaha, but that would simply give her a new place to visit.

She thought that perhaps she shouldn't be obsessing so on the Church, but they did truly aggravate her and she felt they were truly wrong. And that hospital in Florida was on her list as well. Maybe get Cindy to check out that place. Go in for tests and come out dead, definitely not kosher.

She went upstairs to call a couple of old friends and to call about a headstone. She wasn't going to mope.

* * *

Schwartz scheduled a meeting for 1:30 that afternoon for the underwriting staff. Muldoon and the other underwriters figured it would be about something stupid. The office was buzzing about the death of Roundtree by a snake. No one had ever heard of such a thing. Those who knew Roundtree felt bad but still couldn't help but smile when thinking about the encounter. It had to be something to see. They seen events like it in a movie, or seen a snake squeeze some poor animal to death on TV, but not an insurance underwriter. Another first for CMI some thought. *CMI cuts jobs with snake squeezing's.*

It was about one o'clock and Muldoon was hoping to catch Doris in her cubicle. He was in luck she was there.

"You have a minute Doris?"

She looked up and gave him a smile and invited him in. She was seated at her desk with an empty brown paper bag on it and a diet coke. She had just finished eating her lunch and didn't appear to be doing much of anything else. Muldoon took a seat on the vacant chair in the cubicle. He had concerns about her being a supervisor and he being promoted to manager. He was trying to think of a way of approaching the subject without sounding like an idiot. She did seem to disappear quickly after her meeting and he felt it might have been due to what she had just learned. He getting the job over her.

"How are you?"

"I'm fine, why do you ask?"

"I was wondering how you felt about the changes taking place. Bernie being demoted, my taking his place and you being a supervisor under me."

"I thought it was as equals." She said.

"Sorry," he said. "I guess I am the one not use to the new situation."

She looked at him for a minute before responding and tossed the empty bag in the wastepaper basket next to her desk. "To be honest, at first I was kind of aggravated, but the more I thought about it the more I thought well maybe I don't want the grief of being the head person. I kind of feel like Trevayne in a way, just do my job and hope they leave me alone."

"You sure? I know I will really lean on you a lot for some of the things we do."

"That's okay as long as you know the buck stops with you."

Equality must only go so far he thought to himself.

"That's fine with me. I think we can make a good team." This was going a lot easier than he thought it would. Doris was either the most understanding person in the world or perhaps some of Trevayne has rubbed off on her.

"The only thing," he said, "is we are really going to be short of help. With Bernie eventually leaving, Robinson getting ready to leave, and now poor Roundtree not coming back at all it just leaves you, me and Phillips."

"Don't worry we have Tucker."

He was surprised by this as he had no idea what Tucker could do to help.

"You know his wife is the granddaughter of one of the founders of CMI." She told him.

"Really?" He had heard this, but never put much stock in it. What could an old woman do?

"She is also a stockholder."

"Really?" He was starting to sound like a broken record. "I have never heard that much about her."

"It is kind of an interesting story that for whatever reason never has really come to light. Her grandfather who helped find CMI divorced his wife, her grandmother. This happened at about the same time they were starting CMI. The divorce was somewhat bitter as divorces can be at times. Anyway she just wanted to get rid of him. At the time they had one child, an infant. She wanted out of the marriage and be on her way. She supposedly had someone waiting in the wings, which is just rumor.

"She took the daughter and left. The daughter grows up gets married and gives birth to Tucker's wife. The grandfather in the meantime remarries and has a couple of sons and CMI becomes a successful insurance company. When he dies he left his sons some stock and to get back at his first wife he left some to the granddaughter."

"Why not the daughter? That would have been the true heir."

"She and the first wife were dead. Sons eventually sold their stock, took the money and ran so to speak, but the granddaughter for whatever reason kept hers. It is not a hell of a lot of stock but just enough to keep everyone alert. All she wants in return is to live here in Chicago where she was raised, and for her husband to have a well paying good job, which he has."

"Why don't they just fire the dolt, what could she do?"

"Probably not much, but they kept it quiet for this long and now are pretty much in the home stretch. And with all the corporate watchdogs out and about it is best not to call any attention to yourself no matter how innocent. The easy thing to do is sit back and just wait for Tucker to retire or die instead of opening a can of worms and getting a lot of bad publicity. He is in his mid-50's and eventually they will probably offer him a good buyout and he'll take it. Maybe even make her a good offer on her stock."

"What about his kids?"

"One is a doctor believe it or not, considering some of his genes came from Tucker and the daughter married well and spends a good deal of her time in Europe."

"How the hell do you know all this?"

"Lets just say I have my sources." She smiled.

Muldoon looked at Doris and felt it all made sense in a strange way. Muldoon did know Tucker was married, and met his wife. She seemed nice and gave the impression that she didn't care too much about insurance. Just wanted a nice comfortable life, which she did have. Their kids were successful and she probably wanted her husband to be and had the wedge to help him be successful.

"The reason this office is always successful," Doris told him, "is simply CMI makes sure Tucker has good people around him. And if he has one quality, he generally lets people do their job and if you do a good job he will let others know. So basically I am going to hook myself to Tucker's wagon and see where it takes me."

Muldoon was almost speechless. It was all making sense to him. Tucker did have good people around him. Bernie might have been the exception but every barrel on occasion has a bad apple, but now the barrel has been cleaned. The office did make money. And making money is the name of the game. Tucker did pretty much leave his employees alone. Now and then he might butt in on something, like the Jensen file, but that was a rare occurrence and not something that happened on a regular basis.

"So you are going to suck up?" He said to her

"Yep. You know we could suck up together and when he leaves you could be a Branch Manager and I could be the Underwriting Manager. We could still be a team, a very successful team. May even be the prototype for the rest of the company. Just need the right guy to pull a few strings. We could be the model, for what do they call it, oh yeah, *corporate efficiency*." She smiled at him. She did have a nice smile when she let it out.

Muldoon thought she was one sly woman. He wondered what else she knew? She was smart, a hard worker, all their business dealings had been good. He was just going to have to remember that when sucking up he was going to have to watch his back.

He didn't want to be tossed from the wagon.

* * *

It was almost two by the time the meeting began. It was held in a conference room that CMI had off the reception area. There was one long walnut table in the center of the room with 14 chairs around it. The table was shined to a glossy finish. The floor was carpeted. There were three television sets in the room with VCR and CD players as well as a pull down screen and large chalkboard for various presentations.

Schwartz sat at the head of the table with Tucker to his left. The rest of the underwriters, Muldoon, Robinson, Simpson and Phillips were seated with a one-chair cushion between them Schwartz and Tucker. Bernie was not present, as he had already left to see a headhunter to get the job hunt rolling. No one missed him.

"As many of you know," Schwartz started looking around the table, "Larry Muldoon is going to be our new Underwriting Manager. Doris will be our Underwriting Supervisor and we feel this is going to be a very vital and successful team for CMI here in Chicago. We naturally wish them all the success in the world.

"Richards will be going to Omaha." Everyone knew that Bernie would not be going to Omaha but let people believe what they want to believe and say what they want to say.

"Trevayne will be retiring at the end of the year." He turned to Robinson and said, "I personally Trevayne want to thank you for the long and outstanding service you have provided to CMI over the years. You will be missed and almost impossible to replace."

"Thanks you boss."

All eyes turned to Trevayne.

"You all be welcome." Schwartz said. Once a Smoke always a Smoke was all Schwartz could think.

Trevayne was somewhat taken back by Schwartz's response. He naturally assumed the white man would ignore him, but this one didn't. It might be a good time to be getting out.

Schwartz continued. "Right now we are short of help but we will be making efforts to fill the empty underwriting slots as soon as possible."

"How soon?" Phillips wanted to know. This all day work routine was starting to get to him.

There was a knock on the door, and then it opened the receptionist stuck her head in and said, "The police are here."

Quickly four men entered two uniformed policemen and two plain-clothes police.

Those seated around the table were somewhat confused. Finally Tucker said, "What can I do for you?"

"Do you have a John Bosco working here?" It was one of the plainclothesmen, a tall bald guy.

"Yes."

"We want him for questioning."

"My god why?"

"We have evidence that he and a Cyrus Gladkowski have perpetrated or are in the process of committing fraud. We know Gladkowski has and it would appear that Mr. Bosco is part of this little scheme."

"Good God in Heaven." Schwartz said. "Do you know this to be true?"

"Yes, my partner Ira Sampson," he turned to his partner standing next to him, "ran a, shall we say a test on them, and they flunked."

"You need four guys for this?" Tucker asked looking at the four policemen. Seemed like overkill for simply failing a test.

"Better safe than sorry. Now if you can point us to him we will be out of here shortly."

Tucker led the way to Bosco's office with a detour past luscious Vicki Higgins' desk where he slowed and took a deep breath. She looked up from filing her nails and simply ignored him. The police and Schwartz followed him with the underwriters bringing up the rear.

Bosco was on the phone when he looked up and saw Sampson and the police. The blood drained from his face. Sampson then read him his rights and when he was done all the blood was gone. Then the two uniform officers each took an arm and led him out of the office.

The rest of the group simply stood outside the door to Bosco's office watched quietly.

Bosco saw Muldoon, "Get me Cindy," he pleaded.

"She's on her way to Paradise."

"She's dead?" Bosco howled and his knees almost buckled.

"Another death?" Schwartz said. "My god this has been a sad day."

"No she lives there."

"In Paradise?"

"Yeah the one in California."

Tucker watched them take Bosco from the office and wondered if convicted would he have to conduct an exit interview?

TWENTY THREE

Muldoon sat in the upper level on the train ride home to Lombard. This way he did not have to share a seat with anyone. He couldn't believe that he was the Underwriting Manager for the Chicago Office. He was going to call Sarah with the news, not only about the promotion but also the fact that they would not have to move. But by the time Schwartz got through talking about the so called joys of *Corporate Efficiency* and the commotion caused by the arrest of Bosco and the death of Roundtree he had all he could do to make his train. Though he was starting to look forward to going to Omaha the fact that they were staying put was in its own way a relief. He knew Sarah's parents would be happy.

He was looking forward to working with Doris but he reminded himself to keep an eye on her, as she seemed more aware than most of what was going on with CMI. For someone so quiet and perhaps light in the loafers she knew a lot.

His mother would be happy that they would be staying in Chicago. She still had some friends here and no matter what anyone says it is always good to see the old hometown every now and then. Now she could.

The death of Roundtree had him feeling numb. He heard it but didn't feel it. Perhaps with his dad dying in the same week simply drained him of the emotion of losing a friend. Roundtree would have been a nice person to have on board, but they do have Phillips if he could keep him working almost a full day they would have something.

He promised Bosco that he would call Cindy, but he also suggested that there are some good lawyers in Chicago who would be more familiar with the lay of the land than perhaps she would be. But he insisted he wanted her advice for now.

The drive from the train station to their home took about fifteen minutes. It was already dark and there was a cold wind blowing in from the west. He wondered what the weather was like in New York, if it was like it was here, it would take some of the fun out of watching the game, assuming they played. Perhaps New York was even colder.

His mother and Sarah were in the kitchen as he entered. They were both smiling though he knew not why. "I have good news," he announced as he entered. They both looked to him, "I am going to be the new Underwriting Manager for Chicago."

It took awhile for what he said to dawn on Sarah, "you mean we won't have to move."

"Nope."

She came over to him and gave him a hug and a kiss. He gave his mother one. He then told them of his day, the meetings, the untimely death of Roundtree by a snake, which they both found odd, his and Doris's promotions, and the arrest of Bosco.

Sarah couldn't believe that Bosco would do anything like that, "didn't he want to become a priest again."

"I guess that will be put on the back burner for awhile. He wants Cindy to be his lawyer but I think he would be better off with someone local." He said.

"I think they have an office here that may be able to help. Now he will have to get parole as well as an annulment."

"Probably both will cost about the same." Muldoon smiled. Then he thought of Bosco's church. This too had obviously suffered a setback. Muldoon was almost disappointed about that. He was looking forward to it. If nothing else it sounded interesting. Perhaps with a good lawyer he'll beat the rap and be able to start one anyway.

"Sarah has some good news too." His mother said.

Larry looked to her and she gave him a shy smile. "I won a poetry contest," she said.

"Wow, this is our lucky day."

"I won $125.00 from the *Poetry Place* a poetry magazine I read now and then."

"Well let me see it."

"I think you are going to find it is very appropriate," Emily said.

Sarah picked up a folder that was on the counter and handed it to Larry. "It's in here and it will appear in their next month's issue. It is the First Place Winner."

He opened the folder and read the poem.

God had a little money so he gave it to His Son
Go get me some disciples and have a little fun
They ended up with twelve maybe a couple more
Then went house to house looking for some more.

A lot of them of said yes and some of them said no
And some of them of course simply didn't know.
But when that jug of water was turned into sparkling wine
Everyone thought this religion thing was something really fine.

So they did some converting and a little fishing

Casting nets here and there hoping and a wishing

They caught a lot of little ones and now and then a keeper

And every now and then they caught themselves a sleeper

But when they heard of martyrdom some simply started to weep

This was not a promise any wanted to keep.

If you want to die for my sins why that would just be great

But for me to die for yours, well I think you'll have to wait.

So they splintered off some went here and some went there

Some started their own shows just to keep things on the square

But then the rules got complicated it became way too easy to sin

There was just no way the laity was ever going to win.

So now they stay at home and eat some bacon and some eggs

Watch the Sunday talk shows where the politicians lie and beg.

If there is a God, well, no one really knows

But if there really is, He wouldn't do a talk show.

He looked at her and smiled, "Kind of religious."

She smiled back, "Such is life."

Made in the USA
Coppell, TX
03 December 2019